Joyfully Yours,
Jamie
1 Peter 5:7

The Garbage Truck Comes on Tuesdays and Fridays

Throw Your Emotional Garbage Out with the Trash!

Janie Walters

QUAIL RIDGE PRESS

Library of Congress Control Number: 2013958249

ISBN 978-1-934193-99-0
Cover design by Stacey Griffith
Page design by Cynthia Clark
Printed in the United States of America.

QUAIL RIDGE PRESS
P. O. Box 123 • Brandon, MS 39043 • 1-800-343-1583
info@quailridge.com • www.quailridge.com

Dedication

This book is dedicated to Heather, Joseph, and Thomas, my niece and twin great nephews— three children I love with all my heart. My hope for you, and for all of God's children who may one day read this book, is that when challenges confront you, you will face them head-on. When opportunities arise, you will pursue them wisely and fearlessly. When one dream dies, you will have the courage to dream another one. When God grants you great success, you will humbly thank Him and give Him the credit. When skeptics tell you there is no God, may you always have the faith to trust in God, confess Jesus as your Savior—believe that Heaven is real, the Bible is true, and that God really does love you.

Contents

Acknowledgments

To all the people who heard me talk about writing this book for the past ten years, and all the people who patiently asked about my progress, even though I often reported absolutely no progress at all, I say a big THANK YOU! *The Garbage Truck Comes on Tuesdays and Fridays* is now a tangible book, in large part, because of your continuous encouragement.

To Barney and Gwen McKee, the owners and publishers of Quail Ridge Press: Thank you for eagerly embracing the concept of this book and sharing my excitement about its potential for benefiting the lives of hurting people. I pray God will bless you as you have blessed me. Gwen, thanks for giving your expertise to the editing process. *The Garbage Truck Comes on Tuesdays and Fridays* is a better book because of your work.

Thank you to Cyndi Clark and Stacey Griffith for your layout and design of the book's pages and cover. I'm very proud of the way *The Garbage Truck Comes on Tuesdays and Fridays* looks.

To all the staff at Quail Ridge Press (Terresa, Melinda, Lacy, Emily, Shelby, and Holly): Thank you for being true professionals and for embracing this book with enthusiasm, expertise, and excellence.

To Billy Dugger, freelance photographer in Biloxi, Mississippi: Thank you for being the best photographer a girl could ever hope to have as a friend. You do great work!

To my beloved husband Dickie: Even in your death, you continue to help me, providing the most meaningful material of all for this book. Thank you for filling my life with so much love.

Finally, a special "thank you" is given to Jesus, my Lord and Savior. Thanks for Your inspiration and words of wisdom. I hope You like the finished product.

CHAPTER ONE

The Thought That Grew into a Book!

The garbage truck really comes to my house on Tuesdays and Fridays. My husband Dickie and I didn't always keep a spotless house, but we seldom missed taking the trash out on garbage days. Like wedding vows, for richer or poorer, in sickness or in health, we faithfully hauled out the garbage.

Why so vigilant? It's simple. Garbage accumulates! Cans overflow. Contents often rot, and rotting garbage stinks! With that diligence noted, you won't be surprised that the idea for this book was conceived the night before a garbage day.

For some reason—and neither one of us could remember why—Dickie and I were not speaking to each other. We were both swollen like toads, filled with anger about something, and we were not talking! The tension in the atmosphere was so thick dynamite couldn't blast through it, but we had a job to do.

With no sign of surrender in his voice, Dickie came grumping through the house and announced to me, "Janie, it's garbage night." I didn't need a 900-page dissertation to know what to do. We began to collect the garbage from the bedrooms, bathrooms, and kitchen. Once gathered, I pulled the can on wheels to the street, and Dickie carried the recycle bin.

On this particular night as we silently made our way to the street, I thought to myself, "Wouldn't it be nice if Dickie and I could go through our hearts and minds collecting mental and emotional garbage as easily as we went through our house collecting physical garbage? Wouldn't it be nice if somehow we could leave all our hurt feelings beside the street with the rest of the garbage so we could go back into our house as friends?"

Wouldn't it be nice if we could go through our hearts and minds collecting mental and emotional garbage as easily as we went through our house collecting physical garbage?

One of my shortcomings is the strong connection between my mind and mouth. If I think it, I'm likely to say it. If the thought is inspired by the Holy Spirit, this weakness becomes a blessing. But if the devil jumps up in me, my words become a prologue to tragedy.

I decided to risk it. I broke the silence and said, "Dickie darling, wouldn't it be nice if the two of us could go through our hearts and minds, collect all of the mental and emotional garbage that's separating us, put it in a bag, and somehow leave it here on the street, too, so we can go back into our house as friends?"

Much to my delight, Dickie thought it was a grand idea. Without drum roll or fanfare, we stood under the street light and kissed, leaving our "garbage" at the curb. When we went back inside, happiness returned to the Walters' house that night! I was absolutely dumbfounded at how easily and quickly the atmosphere in our home could change. We simply made a decision. We didn't discuss why we felt justified in feeling our different ways. We didn't explain, describe, lament, recap…nothing! We just made a decision to drop it. We dropped it so completely that months later neither one of us could remember what we were arguing about. Tension left the house. Peace and joy returned.

Later, as I reflected on our experience, I wondered, *would this process work in other situations? Could I simply make a decision to drop other negative thoughts, feelings, and experiences with the same results?*

Furthermore, if deciding to drop the negative works for me, would it work for other people? Would it work for them if they were single, instead of married; had different careers than mine; or lived in a different nation, spoke a different language? Would it work regardless of their personalities and thinking styles? What if their faith differed from mine, or if they believed in a different god?

These questions, and others like them, catapulted me into a private study of people—including me—and how we, as fallible human beings, can deal positively with the negatives in our lives.

I was absolutely dumbfounded at how easily and quickly the atmosphere in our home could change. We simply made a decision.

I made note of the vast diversity of negatives we encounter, from broken fingernails, promises, and bones, to lost keys, health, and loved ones, plus everything in between. I considered the various ways people deal with these negatives. I noted the methods that seemed to work, and the ones that seemed only to make matters worse. The result of that study is this book, which has one very simple premise: To live peaceful, happy lives, we must be just as faithful to collect and dispose of mental and emotional garbage as we are to collect and dispose of physical garbage.

Mental and emotional garbage have many of the

same properties of physical garbage. Just like physical garbage, mental and emotional garbage accumulates. Like cans, our hearts and minds often overflow with negativity. The negativity rots inside of us; and, the rotting garbage of negative attitudes, words, and actions always stinks!

To live peaceful, happy lives, we must be just as faithful to collect and dispose of mental and emotional garbage as we are to collect and dispose of physical garbage.

Regular collection times must be established. We must be diligent. We can't wish negatives away. We can't go to bed, pull the covers over us, and expect to awake the next morning to a positive new circumstance. If it were possible, I would have done that on March 22, 2010, the day that began the worst negative of my life.

Peppered throughout this book will be stories of my life and experiences with Dickie Harrison Walters, my husband and best friend for 29 years. On March 22, 2010, Dickie came home from his work at the Federal

Highway Administration and reported he had enjoyed a good day. Though it was 5:30 in the afternoon, the time had recently changed, and the sun was still shining. He decided to go for his usual run before dinner. He dressed in his familiar red running shorts, and out the door he went… never to return. Dickie died of a heart attack during that run. He was only 58 years of age.

Janie and Dickie Walters

That event generated for me a whole galaxy of negatives—so many that one or two trash disposal days were not enough. The garbage had to be hauled out of my heart and mind hourly, sometimes moment by moment.

I was catapulted into a mental, emotional, and spiritual tailspin. I could no longer hold on to God. He had to hold on to me.

That one experience was a graduate-level course in how to neutralize negatives. Through it, I discovered that eliminating negatives requires more than a passing whim. Success requires we make a quality decision to overcome the negative. Once that decision is made, then **we must apply some *powerful cleaning agents* designed specifically for the mind and emotions.** The cleaning strategies offered in this book are:

- Change Your Perspective.

- Practice the Golden Rule.

- Maintain Good Self-Esteem.

- Laugh a Lot.

- Assume Responsibility for Your Feelings.

- Practice the Magic of "Acting As If…"

These powerful cleaning strategies inspired by God and used one at a time or in tandem, have helped me successfully plant my feet on solid mental, emotional, and spiritual ground once again. If they worked for me, I'm confident God will use them to work for you, as well.

However, before we begin, we must first answer the question, "What is garbage?"

CHAPTER TWO

You Call That Garbage?!@#?

What constitutes garbage? Good question! One man's trash can truly be another man's treasure. The old shack you couldn't wait to sell is some young couple's dream home. The motorless jalopy parked in your garage is the prized antique that quickly sells on eBay.

The same can be said of mental and emotional garbage. What aggravates you and sends you into a tailspin doesn't bother someone else at all. As a matter of fact, they can't understand why you get so upset. The obstacles and competitions that cause you to lose sleep at night are the very things that give another person's life meaning and purpose. They live to tackle them.

So, how do we define garbage? Depending on our perspective, even good things can become garbage. Dickie and I never argued much, and the extent of the arguments usually included only a word or two here, a silence there, a flash of a look yonder, and poof… argument over. But garbage was actually the cause of several of our disagreements. The items I wanted to throw away, Dickie wanted to keep—and vice versa!

One such argument occurred over magazines. Dickie and I both enjoyed magazines—neither one of us would have classified them as *garbage*—but neither one of us had a lot of time to read them. Realizing how quickly magazines accumulate around the house, I deliberately let some of my subscriptions expire.

Depending on our perspective, even good things can become garbage.

Having made this prudent sacrifice, I noticed Dickie had not followed suit. In particular, he continued to subscribe to two travel magazines, both of which he rarely opened. Every month the stack of unread magazines on our coffee table grew. When the twelfth one arrived, I took the whole stack to the garage, intending to take them to some school or doctor's office.

I was surprised Dickie even noticed the stack was gone, but when he discovered what I wanted to do with the magazines, the debate was furious, though its conclusion was simple: What I viewed as garbage— magazines that covered a large portion of the table and collected dust from nonuse—Dickie viewed as important. He reasoned that though he may never go to some of the travel destinations—or even read about them—the presence of the magazines left his options open and the thoughts available. What was garbage to me was not garbage to Dickie. Consequently, I didn't take the magazines anywhere. I left them on a shelf in the garage where they remained until three years after his death. Yes, smiling ever so slightly, I finally threw them in the recycle bin.

If we can't recognize garbage, how will we ever be able to eliminate it?

So, we're back to the question, *"What is garbage?"* Because we sometimes have trouble identifying physical garbage, *how will we ever know what constitutes something as intangible as mental and emotional garbage?* Furthermore, if we can't recognize it, how will we ever be able to eliminate it?

This is the only place in the book I will attempt to define the essence of garbage, a.k.a. negativity! **The Garbage Truck Comes on Tuesdays and Fridays is designed to help maximize life's positives by**

providing simple suggestions for *eliminating* the negatives, not focusing on them. However, eliminating negative garbage is difficult when we're not even sure what it is!

If you are confident you already know all aspects of the "garbage" you are dealing with, and you want to jump directly into my suggested cleaning agents, then skip this section, and start with Chapter Four. The rest of you are invited to stay with me as we seek foundational answers to this complex question: What is garbage?

As I see it, only two types of garbage exist:

- Things we originally wanted, but have now lost their usefulness to us.

- Things we never asked for, but must contend with anyway.

The simplest definition of garbage is "anything that has lost its usefulness." This assumes a time existed when an item, an experience, a thought, action, emotion—or whatever—was useful to us…we wanted it and accepted it into our lives as something good, desirable, or necessary. Now, however, that "something" has arrived at a point where it is no longer useful or good for us.

Examples of this definition in the physical world are plentiful. The pork 'n' beans originally needed a can;

the eggs needed a carton; the groceries needed a sack. However, when the beans and eggs are eaten, and the groceries are put away, the can, carton, and sack become garbage.

This definition doesn't imply that our garbage is no longer useful to anyone. Admittedly, the can, carton, and sack can be recycled or used in creative ways. Share them, if you like. Much physical garbage can be recycled, even stinking things like shrimp shells and toxic things, like used motor oil. The definition just means that this "something" is no longer of value to us.

Thoughts and emotions of grief, anger, fear, or frustration are not inherently wrong. Each initially serves a worthwhile purpose.

Our definition—something that has lost its usefulness—has mental and emotional implications, as well. Thoughts and emotions of grief, anger, fear, or frustration are not inherently wrong. Each initially serves a worthwhile purpose. Thoughts help us define an experience and determine the experience's impact on our lives. Emotions become like shock absorbers, softening the internal jolt of an external experience. The problem comes when we hold on to these troubling thoughts and emotions too long, or improperly dispose of them with negative thinking, talking, and actions. When we do this, we produce negativism, a.k.a. mental and emotional garbage.

Consider these examples: When a cherished loved one dies, we grieve. When we get laid off from our jobs, we feel insecure. When a drunk driver injures our child, we become angry. These negative emotions should not be called garbage. They are normal, natural responses to negative experiences. However, when grieving leads us to withdraw from people, or makes us sick, we have held on to the grief too long. When insecurity over a lost job leads us to abuse drugs and/or alcohol, we've improperly dealt with that emotion. Likewise, when anger over a hurt child causes us to take the law into our own hands, we have perverted anger's use. Remember, we're defining mental and emotional garbage that has lost its usefulness to us.

The week after Dickie died, I was numb. Because we had no children, and he had no siblings, planning the funeral, notifying all the people, and seeing to the details of the burial were my sole responsibility. After all the people returned home and I was left alone, grief moved in…and stayed with me for many months. I cried the proverbial river. I was the epitome of being "down in the dumps," and I established residence in the depths of many of them.

To move forward, we must deliberately turn from the negative thoughts, words, and actions and go in a different direction.

I methodically moved through each day, devoid of any positive emotions, filled only with grief, sadness, and dread. As strange as it sounds, those months of darkness were helpful to me. They helped me process a great loss, and maneuver through a major life change. On March 9, 2010, I was a happily married woman, looking forward to a summer of fun and travel. Twenty-four hours later, I was a widow—a title I never once thought about owning. In a moment, the outside, tangible parts of my life on earth had changed, while the insides of my heart and mind were in major revolt. **The many tears served as a release valve that allowed some of that internal stress to escape.**

Over time, the expression of those negative emotions helped me settle into my new reality. Finally, a day came when I was tired of being sad. I was tired of tear-smeared mascara in public places. The emotions had accomplished their purpose. I decided if I was to live, I wanted the remaining days of my life to be happy, not sad. This turning point in my grief took months to reach. Some people reach a similar decision in a few weeks…others take years.

Regardless of how long it takes, **when we have adjusted internally to the shock of the experience, we've reached the maximum good a negative emotion can provide.** To move forward, we must deliberately turn from the negative thoughts, words, and actions and go in a different direction. When a negative emotion renders its maximum good, we must "take it to the curb!" The sooner we can do this, the better off we are.

Remember, garbage, by definition, falls into one of two categories:

- Anything that has lost its usefulness.

- Things we never ask for, but must contend with anyway.

The earth is peppered with examples of garbage we didn't request. I'm talking about the wildfire that destroys everything in its path; the rains that flood your house; the hail that beats your crops into the ground.

This garbage comes from the uncontrollable atmosphere, blind-siding you, and leaving you dazed.

Despicable physical garbage can come from nowhere, too. The cancer just appears. You eat right, exercise, don't smoke, but the disease appears. Fear, dread, and uncertainty flood your mind. Major garbage!

You looked both ways, but before you cleared the intersection, the 18-wheeler plowed right into you. You're facing a totaled car and a long hospital stay. You might lose your job. Pain, anger, frustration, and worry haunt your heart. Major garbage, yes, but insurmountable, no!

Thankfully, all experiences—even ones we didn't request—will eventually come to an end. To eliminate garbage, we must have the courage to look past the here-and-now to what lies beyond the experience…what lies weeks, months, years from now at the end of it. **Seeing the end initiates our power to be positive.**

The bottom line is this: Regardless of how trivial or tragic the unrequested garbage is, if we think negative thoughts, say negative words, and perform negative actions, we absolutely create for ourselves a negative attitude, and perpetuate a negative life, giving far more power to that one experience than it warrants. We let the negative define us!

Conversely, if we think positive thoughts, say positive words, and perform positive actions, we create for ourselves the potential of limiting the devastating effects of the experience, producing instead a positive attitude, and perpetuating a positive life. This way, we let the positives define us!

If we want to live a positive life, we must, I repeat, we *must* kick our garbage to the curb!

In the midst of our most unwanted situations, we have the opportunity to choose. Do we want to live a positive, happy life, or don't we? If we want to live a positive life, we must, I repeat, we *must* kick our garbage to the curb! How long will you tarry between two opinions? Like Moses challenged the children of Israel in their commitment to God, "I place before you life and death. Choose life…."[1]

You don't need a wealth of resources to generate an acceptable ending to a negative experience. **One positive thought is all it takes to turn a negative experience around.** One positive thought… one word spoken with confidence…one action taken in faith…can catapult any soul from hopelessness to hopefulness.

In summary, what is garbage? Physical, mental, or emotional garbage consists of anything that has lost its usefulness, or things that never had any usefulness—garbage we didn't want, but must contend with anyway!

Physical, mental, or emotional garbage consists of anything that has lost its usefulness, or things that never had any usefulness—garbage we didn't want, but must contend with anyway!

Taking out the trash regularly at our homes is simple, but what must we do to rid ourselves of mental and emotional garbage? That answer is simple, too: **Make a quality decision to move forward. Decide *you want to be happy*. Decide to *be an overcomer*.** Decide *not to get bogged down in the negatives of the past or the present.* Rather, decide to use the positives you can identify to design for yourself an *optimistic plan for the future*, then pursue it.

I hope at this point you hear yourself saying, "Janie, I'm ready to make a quality decision. I want to let go of what lies behind and press on to what lies ahead.[2] I'm asking God to create within me a clean heart, free of garbage, and renew a right spirit within me.[3] Plus, I want to enjoy life's journey. Please tell me how. How do I make a quality decision that will rid me of mental and emotional garbage?"

If these are things you hear your heart saying, then prepare yourself for a fun-filled adventure! The rest of this book contains proven trash-removing tools— "powerful cleaning agents"—to help us de-clutter and disinfect our hearts and minds. Peppered throughout these cleaning agents will be lessons we can learn from garbage. I call them **Trash Can Truths**. Pause periodically, and think on them.

Now let's move to the question, "How do we make a quality decision?" Get ready! We haven't much time! *The Garbage Truck Comes on Tuesdays and Fridays.*

CHAPTER THREE

A Decision IS Only as Good as the Action That Supports It!

According to *Consumer Reports*, May 2012, Glad Drawstring Stronger–With-Less-Plastic, and Hefty The Gripper are the top-rated garbage bags, each able to carry 50 pounds of barbells without breaking. Some cheaper brands break with only 35 pounds of barbells.[1] I don't know about you, but I don't skimp when purchasing garbage bags. Likewise, whether the emotional garbage is created by a rude driver on the freeway, a boss who reprimands harshly, or something more severe, collecting our garbage requires a quality bag, a.k.a. a quality decision.

You see, we have many options when responding to a negative. We can ask ourselves:

- Do we want to cry, pout, and feel sorry for ourselves?

- Do we want to get even or blame someone else?

- Do we want to fret, regret, or get angry about it?

- Do we want to analyze, justify, criticize, compare, bemoan, magnify, ignore, forget, or just live with it?

We have the freedom to do any of the above. The experience now belongs to us. Life has given it to us. Take heart; you are not somehow deviant if you initially feel like engaging in all of the above. Go ahead. It's your experience and your life.

Hopefully, the day will quickly come when you grow tired of the stench of negativity. When that blessed day comes, declare, "Today is garbage day! I'm emptying my cans!" Say it out loud. Announce it to someone!

As momentous as this declaration is in the life of a decision, nevertheless, garbage will remain in the can (or our minds and hearts) until the can is emptied. Zig Ziglar, the beloved motivational speaker and author of *See You at the Top*, and numerous other inspirational books, explained why this is true in the following example: Five birds are sitting on a fence. Three birds decide to fly away. How many birds does that leave on the fence? Those who have never heard the riddle have a tendency to answer "two." However, Mr. Ziglar told his audience the answer is "five," with the explanation being that deciding to fly and actually flying are two different things.[2]

Likewise, deciding to eliminate mental and emotional garbage requires more than just saying it. Cheap garbage bags, like ordinary decisions made with only words, easily burst. Action is the component that distinguishes a quality decision from an ordinary one. Many people proudly announce they're going on a diet Monday morning, and they're off the diet by noon! The four-step process that renders a quality decision is simple:

- Think about what you want to do.

- Make a commitment in your heart to do it.

- State your intentions out loud.

- Take action. **Do something!**

The following story illustrates this process. Years ago, one of the deepest hurts I experienced was a divorce. I was a Christian, a good girl, well educated, and "it wasn't supposed to happen to me." As far as I knew, I had been a good wife. Yet, after only twenty months of marriage, I heard the words, "I don't love you anymore. I want a divorce." Like millions of people across the country and around the world, I toured through a gallery of emotions, a trip that gratefully came to an abrupt end during a dramatic scene.

Sitting on my sofa one Friday night, I began to cry. I cried so hard I fell off the sofa onto the floor, crumpled, blubbering and whimpering for at least ten minutes. I came to my senses when I noticed my tears, slobber, and snot were getting all over the carpet.

Cheap garbage bags, like ordinary decisions made with only words, easily burst.

I sat up straight and said out loud, "Janie, you are made of better stuff than this. You serve a greater God and come from stronger stock. You're not the first person to get divorced, and you won't be the last. You have just shed your last tear over this fiasco, little girl! Now, get up, wash your face, and *clean up this mess!*"

I did exactly that. Without even realizing it, I followed the formula I've outlined for you. I thought about what I wanted to do, made a commitment in my heart to do it, announced it out loud, then got up and took some positive action. I moved beyond the hurt, and I've never looked back.

Perhaps because the climax was so dramatic, or because twenty months wasn't a lifetime of memories to overcome, bagging the garbage of my divorce didn't take repeated effort on my part; however, that is not true with all of my garbage.

Mental and emotional garbage is often so deeply buried in our hearts, repeated cleaning efforts are needed. **The need for repeated action to neutralize a negative does not indicate weakness in our character or a lack of resolve in our decision. Some hurts simply penetrate down to the very bottom of our souls.** God knew this when He created us. He gave us the instruction to ask—and keep on asking; to knock—and keep on knocking; to seek—and keep on seeking. He promised that if we would persist, we would eventually receive, doors would eventually open, and we would eventually find what we're seeking.[3] This principle works well on garbage.

I remember the time I was invited to speak for my first "Fortune 100" company. The occasion was a banquet, and I was their keynote speaker. This was a wonderful opportunity to move into a larger market. If I performed well, I was confident the CEO would give me a good letter of recommendation that could open many doors.

I wanted to impress them. I did extra research, found fresh material, and enthusiastically stepped onto the platform. I had been instructed to speak for about thirty minutes. To help monitor my time, an employee volunteered to signal me when I had five minutes left.

The audience and I were laughing and having a great time. I was thrilled with the way things were going, until I glanced and saw the stern look from the CEO. I knew something was wrong but wasn't sure what. I quickly ended the speech and only afterwards discovered my mistake. The lady either forgot to signal me, or I missed it. I spoke fifteen minutes too long.

Mental and emotional garbage is often so deeply buried in our hearts, repeated cleaning efforts are needed.

I felt terrible and was so disappointed with myself. Though I would have loved to point the finger of blame, I knew the mistake was ultimately mine.

I tried to apologize—an action intended to put the lid on the CEO's dissatisfaction—but he didn't seem to accept my apology. The lid popped off my can, and the garbage reeked! I had been given a great opportunity, and I blew it.

This heaviness of heart stayed with me on and off for weeks. Because I'm a Christian, the first place I run when trouble hits me is to God. I took repeated positive actions. I prayed, read my Bible, accepted forgiveness from God, confessed that He would make this work together for my good, and tried to deliberately think and say good things.

I did everything I knew to do, but still the depressing regret lingered. No matter what I tried, the awful smell kept emanating from the can. Finally, I took one significant action that purged the hurt forever.

Even though I immediately started thinking and saying right things and taking right actions, once was not enough. Persistence was required.

At Christmastime, I send gifts to my clients, thanking them for the opportunity to serve with them during the year. Usually, I just mail the gift to the person who contacted me and paid me. (Though I tend to like all the people in an organization, I have a special appreciation for those who pay me!)

When it came to this client, I felt led to send a gift to the CEO, as well as to my initial contact. As I placed his gift in the mail, I visualized myself releasing all the hurt associated with him. I said out loud, **"I forgive you for your failure to forgive me, and I pray that this gift brings with it God's blessings on your life."** As I walked away from the post office, I realized for the first time since the event, my heart seemed lighter. My outlook seemed brighter. I knew I had truly done all I could do. I had arrived at peace.

Notice, even though I immediately started thinking and saying right things and taking right actions, once was not enough. Persistence was required. When one thing didn't work, I tried something else. **You see, the quality decision dictated I could not stop until the garbage was eliminated.** Because of persistence, that mental and emotional garage was on the street Friday morning—tightly secured in the can—awaiting the truck.

That's how it works, folks. To make a quality decision, just think about what you want to do, make a commitment in your heart to do it, state your intentions out loud, and take action. Keep acting until the negative is mastered. Now, on to our powerful cleaning agents! Get ready to eliminate some garbage and haul it to the street!

CHAPTER FOUR

Cleaning Agent #1:
Change Your Perspective

Trash Can Truth #1

It takes 197,215,920 eight-inch plastic water bottles to wrap around the world one time.[1]

For years we watched the city dump fill with treadless tires, empty jelly jars, yesterday's newspapers, plastic bottles, and Vienna sausage cans. Those items were our garbage. Then our perspective on garbage changed.

Someone discovered we could recycle glass, plastic, paper, aluminum, rubber, and the like. Those items could be reduced, remolded, and reused. Our garbage has never been the same. What was once useless trash has now become a thriving business. Because of recycling, we learned to look at garbage a new way. We changed our perspective.

Changing our perspective is a wonderful way of recycling mental and emotional garbage, too. Simply defined, *changing our perspective* means that we take garbage, find something worthwhile in it, and focus our attention on the worthwhile. We find a positive way to look at a negative.

Focusing on the positives in a bad situation doesn't always eliminate the negative, but it does help minimize the negative's toxic effects. Face it! Some problems just won't go away!

Simply defined, changing our perspective means . . . we find a positive way to look at a negative.

The story is told of one father who tried to get his four-year-old son ready for bed. The child first ignored him, then spit toothpaste all over the bathroom countertop, and kicked and twisted when the father tried to put pajamas on him. Finally, after getting his son in bed, the father sat down to read his evening newspaper.

Five minutes passed, and then the father heard, "Daddy, I'm thirsty. Would you bring me a glass of water?" The father said, "No! You could have had all the water you wanted if you would have cooperated, but you didn't, so I'm not bringing you any water."

Five more minutes passed and the boy said, "Daddy, would you please bring me a glass of water?" The father relied, "No! You heard what I said. Now don't ask me again. If you do, I'm going to come in there and spank you!"

Five short minutes later the boy said, "Daddy, when you come in here to spank me, will you bring me a glass of water?!" Like I said, some problems just won't go away!

While I find humor in that story, real life examples of negatives that won't go away are everywhere.

- **Example:** You accidentally dropped your wedding ring in the Atlantic Ocean—the ring your husband had made with diamonds from his mother's ring. Cry all you want. Grieve over the loss for months, but you're not going to find that ring or ever be able to duplicate its sentimental value. So, what to do? **Change your perspective.** You're still married, and you enjoyed the ring while you had it.

- **Example:** Your oldest child got caught embezzling money from his company, and is spending the next two years in prison without parole. You're shocked, embarrassed, angry, and disappointed. You can mope around and cry for two years if you want to, or you can change your perspective. So your son made a mistake. Maybe he learned a valuable lesson that will make him a better man. Regardless, he's still alive, you know where he is, and you can visit him.

Most situations contain more than one truth.

Changing our perspective doesn't mean we deny or ignore the truth of an experience—the corporation *is* losing money; the boss *is* a micromanager; you haven't had a date in months, etc. That may be the truth of our current garbage. Most situations, however, contain more than one truth. When dealing with negatives, always look again. If you want to find happiness in the midst of the mess, try to change your perspective, and see positive truths that most certainly exist.

People generally don't like to change, but the adage is true: If we keep doing what we've been doing, we'll keep getting the same results.

The joke is told of a man who went to a doctor complaining his ears were ringing, and his eyes felt like they were going to pop right out of his head. The first doctor told him it was his teeth…they all needed to be pulled. So he had his teeth pulled, but the problem persisted. He went to a second doctor, and explained his ears were ringing and his eyes felt like they were going to pop right out of his head. This doctor said it was his tonsils…they needed to be removed. So he had his tonsils removed, but the problem persisted. Finally a third doctor diagnosed his condition as terminal. The man was told he only had six months to live.

Insanity: Doing the same thing over and over again and expecting different results.—Albert Einstein

---

"Six months," he thought. "Well, if I only have six months, I'm going to live it up!" He cashed in his CDs and took all the money out of his bank account. He then rented a penthouse apartment, hired a chauffeur to take him anywhere he wanted to go, and went to a tailor to have his clothes custom made—something he'd always wanted to do.

The tailor was measuring him for his shirts and said out loud, "Sleeve…34 inches. Neck…16 inches." The gentleman corrected him and said, "Oh, no, Sir. My neck size is size 15. You'll need to re-measure." The tailor complied but still reported, "Sir, your neck size is 16 inches." The man became irate. He demanded, "I've lived my entire adult life wearing shirts size 15 in the neck, and I'll be buried in a neck size of 15!"

The tailor apologized and said, "As you would like it, Sir. I'll make your shirts with 15-inch necks; but if your ears start ringing and your eyes start feeling like they're going to pop right out of your head, don't blame me!"

We're so often like this man with the growing neck. Our defiant spirit says, "This is the way I see it, the way I've always seen it, the way it's going to be! I have rights, and you can't make me change my perspective."

To that spirit I say, "You're correct! You have a right to see your situation any way you want to see it. But **if your current perspective is depressing your spirit, crippling your attitude, making your body weak, limiting your future options, and polluting the atmosphere for those around you, you might at least consider changing your perspective!**"

Someone reading this book is saying, "Janie, my situation is the exception to the rule. No positives exist."

Please don't take the easy way out. Your future joy and happiness are at stake.

This cleaning agent is about eliminating—or at least neutralizing—negatives by changing your perspective toward them...searching for the good in a situation while treading water in an ocean of negatives. Perspective is about hanging on to that good once you find it, however small it is, and letting "the good" buoy you in the storm. Admittedly, good perspectives are not always obvious. Finding them is often hard work. Holding on to them is even harder.

On occasions people have shared their negative experiences with me, and I'm speechless...totally grieved, and for the moment, incapable of seeing anything good.

- When your child is one of the students shot to death by a twisted teenager high on heroin in your neighborhood school, good is not obvious.

- When a hurricane hits your coastal shores and you lose your house and everything you own, including some family members, good is not obvious.

- When a computer crashes destroying weeks of documented work, good is not always obvious.

Don't despair, however. **A good perspective is always an option.** *No exceptions exist!* **When you cannot see any good in a situation, then look for the Abiding Good.** In a May 2011 Gallup Poll, more than nine out of ten Americans still say "Yes" when asked the basic question, "Do you believe in God?"[2] I am one of those "nine."

Perspective is about hanging on to that good once you find it, however small it is, and letting "the good" buoy you in the storm.

The first Bible principle I learned as a child was "God is good."[3] This good God promised He would be with us even unto the end of the world.[4] God promised we would find Him if we searched for Him with all of our hearts.[5]

Faith is defined as "the substance of things hoped for; the *evidence of things not seen.*"[6] We don't have to see God to know He is there. In the midst of overwhelming negatives, our work is to have faith and believe.[7] As time passes, and the events of negative experiences unfold and play themselves out, the positive treasures hidden in negatives generally become more obvious. In hindsight, we'll be able to see more clearly.

I practice what I preach! My first husband divorced me. I did not want the divorce, and fought to stop it, but failed. I quickly looked for some good in that failure, and found it. Divorce made me single again and available when Dickie Walters came along. Dickie was a much more loving husband to me, and helped me create an exciting and wonderful life.

Believe that though your world seems to be hurling out of control, God is still in control of it.

The Bible teaches us that "Anyone who comes to God must believe that He is, and that He is a rewarder of those who diligently seek Him."[8] When you cannot see good in a bad situation and none of your friends or counselors can point you to any, that's when you need to run to this scripture. Grab hold of it with your mind, and don't let go.

Believe with your heart that God really is…that He really does exist. Believe that though your world seems to be hurling out of control, God is still in control of it. Believe that He will eventually reward you with inner peace and power for living, and a positive perspective on your nightmare. I couldn't be writing this book if I hadn't believed this during the weeks and months following Dickie's death.

Thankfully, not all human garbage revolves around death and ruin. **Many everyday situations steal joy: deadlines, difficult people, flat tires, hate-your-job attitudes, kids out of control, and gum on your shoe. When it comes to this type of trash that is common to man, perspective is a powerful cleaning agent.**

One man succeeded at using perspective well. The story is told of a 70-year-old man who was engaged to be married to a 25-year-old lady. His friends were appalled. They said the age difference was too great. His friends chastised him saying, "You know these May and December weddings never work. Oh, we know what you're going to get out of the marriage. You're going to get a breath of spring; but, what is this young chick going to get out of it?" The 70-year-old gent answered, "CHRISTMAS!" He was focusing on the positive aspects of the potentially lopsided relationship.

We can do the same. If we don't like what we see

in our relationships—and we can't change the people—then we need to find a new way of seeing them.

Dickie was a runner. That's a step faster than a jogger, for those of you who don't follow the sport. He habitually came straight in from work, donned his running clothes, and hit the streets. After several miles of running, he'd return home, exercise, and cool down. We could never be anywhere before 7:00 in the evening, and dinner was rarely served before 8:00 p.m.

We can change our thinking, which will change our perspective.

As a young bride, this drove me nuts. I would come home from work and cook a delicious dinner, eager to be a good wife. Then, I would sit and watch the food get cold while Dickie finished his ritual. No amount of pleading and pouting on my part altered his schedule.

We were married for 29 years. I would have spent much of that time frustrated had I not changed my perspective.

Instead of deciding Dickie was inconsiderate for not abiding by my time schedule, I chose to be proud of the fact he was committed to physical fitness. I chose to marvel at his dedication, and I still long to be as dedicated to anything as he was to running.

The same principle can be applied to every experience in our lives, including the following examples. During any experience, we can change our thinking, which will change our perspective.

Experience: I lose my job.

> **Negative thoughts:** I won't have any money coming in. I may not be able to pay my bills.

> **Positive thoughts:** I might get a better job, or learn a new skill, or see a new part of the country, should I need to move.

Experience: The doctor's prognosis is bad. I have six months to live.

> **Negative thoughts:** I don't want to die. Life is not fair.

> **Positive thoughts:** God can override the doctor's report. If He doesn't, thankfully I have time to get my affairs in order. Think of the people who die instantly from accidents and heart attacks with no time to prepare for anything.

Experience: Your loved one dies instantly, with no time to prepare!

> **Negative thoughts:** This is not fair. Life is unjust. I don't know where anything is.

> **Positive thoughts:** I'm so grateful my loved one didn't have to suffer. I am smart and will be just fine.

This last example was written from my life. In addition to these thoughts, I rejoiced because Dickie was a Christian. He's running on streets of gold in Heaven… no allergies, no bills to pay. Best yet, I'll see him again!

Trash Can Truth #2

The average American discards 4.43 pounds of garbage each day.[9]

At times in my life, I've been deliriously happy and morosely sad—I like happy much better. Most people do. Sad is not fun. I agree whole-heartedly with Chuck Swindoll who says, "Life is 10% what happens to me, and 90% how I react to it."[10] Regardless of what is going on in our lives, people generally want to get up when knocked down. Perspective is helping ourselves get up!

Even when the new perspective you find cannot compare in magnitude to the negative you have encountered, if you hang on long enough, that small, insignificant positive word, like a tiny rudder on a huge ship, can turn your entire mental and emotional condition around.[11]

I'm reminded of the story of Elijah, a prophet in Israel who prayed that no rain would fall in the land for three years, and God answered that prayer. After three and a half years, the land was dry and barren. Elijah once again prayed—this time asking God to send rain.

As Elijah prayed for rain, he sent his servant seven times, commanding him, "Go and look out toward the sea. Report to me any sign of rain." Six times the servant went and saw nothing. Finally, the seventh time his servant reported, "I saw a little cloud the size of a man's hand rising from the sea." Before long that little cloud turned the whole sky black, and a terrific rainstorm came.[12]

Just like Elijah and his servant, times will come when we look for something good in our bad experience and see nothing—but keep looking. Practice your faith walk. Keep on believing, and keep on searching. The good you finally discover may be small, but give it a chance to grow. Focus specifically on that good. Nourish it by being thankful for finding it.

I once completed a two-month, grueling schedule of presentations. On the front end, I was thrilled at the opportunities before me. My energy was high. I then logged 5,000 miles on the road, dozens of speeches, a recording session, many nights in motel rooms, and interaction with hundreds of people. Driving home from my last engagement, I knew I'd pushed too hard and gone too far. The car was on cruise control. I sat mindlessly behind the wheel, starring straight head, numb to my surroundings. I was physically tired and emotionally spent. The motivator was slap out of motivation. I had become negative. That's the truth.

**I don't care how tired, depressed,
or defeated you may be;
always look again for another truth,
however small it might be!**

The truth is I was about as close to giving up and quitting as I had ever been in my career. I had thoughts like, *Let's sell the house and downsize; let's move to a small community, plant some tomatoes, and watch* Wheel of Fortune *in the evenings like normal people. Let's live on less and expect less and do less. With any luck, we'll die soon and all of this going and doing will be over.* That's the truth.

Though I did indeed have these thoughts, when I

sought to change my perspective—when I took the time to look again—I saw a new truth. I don't care how tired, depressed, or defeated you may be; always look again for another truth, however small it might be!

In this instance, I chose to look back over the past two months and focus on the positive things I believed I had accomplished. I compiled quite an impressive list, none of which would have happened had I stayed safely at home.

**Anytime we can learn something
from an experience,
the experience was valuable.**

In those two months, I produced a new training tool that I truly believed would be helpful to all types of organizations going through change. I mentored several people who wanted to become professional speakers; I helped hundreds of people earn CEU credits toward certification in their chosen fields; and I encouraged scores of people to strive for the best life has to offer, and encouraged them to give their best back to life. The truth is my life had made a difference for good in those two months, even though the "good" was, for the most part, intangible. Just knowing the work was not in vain was a positive perspective I could grasp.

When all else fails, fall back on this small but significant perspective: Anytime we can learn something from an experience, the experience was valuable. When I looked again at my recent travel, I learned a valuable lesson. I am an exhaustible unit with limits. I need to discover those limits and become wise about scheduling.

I also embraced the truth that God has a call on my life. He has equipped me with a unique message, packaged that message in a unique person, and sent me to unique people…people in need specifically of the message He's given me for them.

Motivational speakers number in the thousands. Motivational books are published by the tens of thousands. Yet, someone exists who needs to hear this message from my story. They don't own every book, but they will, by hook or crook, have this one in their hands. **This book may just become their map back to fun!**

Trash Can Truth #3

When cleaning your kitchen after a party,
check your garbage for silverware.

Quitting, giving up, and throwing away something valuable during negative experiences are common mistakes. **People often unknowingly toss good things into the garbage.** The first time I used my sterling silver flatware, a small bread knife covered with food was accidentally tossed into the trash and never recovered. My mother's bottom denture—wrapped in a paper napkin—went out in the nightly garbage and had to be replaced. Realizing that it's possible to throw valuable things away by accident, be careful. Don't make the mistake of throwing away an otherwise good marriage, job, school, or life. When you can't eliminate the negative, seek a new perspective that helps you at least make the best of it.

Let's apply this cleaning agent to one more example. On average, one in four Americans will be told they have cancer this year. We're talking about big-time garbage—not good news. No one wants to hear it. Cancer is a diagnosis that plunges people into the depths of despair.

When cancer first began appearing in startling numbers, our treatments were haphazard, and our surgeries were clumsy. The survival rate was low. That's the truth.

Don't make the mistake of throwing away an otherwise good marriage, job, school, or life.

However, in the years that have followed, American ingenuity and research have been applied to this disease—data has been collected, laboratories built, medicines developed. We have made advances in our war against cancer. A new truth now exists.

Today, thanks to early detection, even though a large number of people still develop cancer, more people survive the disease than die from it. Did you hear me?

More people are living with and surviving cancer today than dying with it! The odds have tilted in our favor![13] That's the truth!

Now, should we hear the diagnosis, we have a decision to make. What truth will we focus on and believe? What truth will we hold on to and confess? I'm not *Pollyanna*. My friends Nell and Edwina maintained great attitudes with optimistic, faith-filled confessions. Both died of cancer. A positive perspective did not cure them. However, even if we become one of the many who still lose our battle with cancer, **a positive perspective ranks us among those who win at living.** We have at least spent our last days hopeful and joyful instead of defeated and sorrowful. Our perspective becomes our memorial.

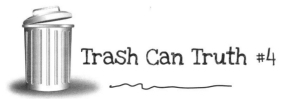

Trash Can Truth #4

In British English, a garbage bag is called
a bin bag or bin liner.

Perspective is more than just seeing something differently; it's talking differently about that something as well. By simply changing a name, we can elevate a job description; by changing a word, we can alter an attitude. Using this approach to perspective, garbage collectors become waste management specialists…and a nagging wife becomes a persistent lady!

Many people reading this book believe God created the world, not with a cosmic bang, but with the spoken word. "And God said…."[14] We also believe human beings are created in the image of God.[15] Thus, like Him, we can create our worlds every day by the words we speak. Even secular psychology teaches us our words become "self-fulfilling prophesies."

Prophesying good into our future can be as simple as managing our words—exchanging defeated words for victory words and pain words for power words. Instead of saying, "I can't," say, "I can." Instead of saying, "It's a problem," acknowledge that every problem is an opportunity to grow and learn. Life's not a struggle. Life is a great adventure!

Recognizing verbal garbage is easy. The words are full of doubt and despair.

Furthermore, don't "awfulize" a situation—a phenomenon identified in Denis Waitley's book, *Seeds of Greatness*. According to Waitley, we say phrases like, "I'm half-dead," instead of simply saying, "I'm tired." We say catastrophic instead of unfortunate; devastated instead of discouraged; and furious instead of disappointed.[16]

The problem is that these exaggerated words hurt us. Right now, while you're reading this book, say out loud the word "furious." Come on. Put the concept to the test. Say the word "furious" with the kind of energy we normally use when we say it in frustration and anger.

"Furious!" Did you notice the many changes that took place in your body when you said the word?

If you're like me, you wrinkled your brow, tightened your lips, and tensed your throat and chest, setting off a whole chain of negative chemical reactions—enough, if sustained, to give you a headache and cause insomnia! After a day of saying, "The heat is sweltering…I've got tons of reports to do…I'm literally buried under a mountain of paperwork, and my head is about to explode…" is it any wonder we fall in bed at night totally exhausted?

Trash Can Truth #5

Garbage Out—Garbage In!

You must have known that phrase would appear some-where in the book, but you're probably thinking, "Janie, you've got it backwards. Doesn't it go, "Garbage in— garbage out?" When applied to words, this phrase, as stated, exemplifies the whole vocabulary issue.

When I go through my house collecting garbage, I know while I'm doing it, more garbage will soon take its place, always coming in from somewhere. Likewise, when we speak garbage out loud, we hear ourselves say it, thus guaranteeing that more garbage will enter our ears by the sound of our own voice. **Garbage out of our mouths comes into our ears.**

Verbal garbage includes negative self-talk. Sentences

like: "No one likes me. I can't do anything right. I'm fat. Ugly was birthed on my face and sprouted throughout my body."

Verbal garbage isn't limited to self-talk. Other people spew garbage on us, too. Comments like: "You're a waste of my time. You're pathetic. You're never going to amount to anything. I wish you'd never been born."

We must be diligent in monitoring the words we speak and uprooting from our psyches poisonous words planted there by others.

Recognizing verbal garbage is easy. The words are full of doubt and despair: "It's impossible. You might as well give up. No one will ever help you." And on a broader scale: "The economy is a mess. The government's collapsing. The planet is melting. There's no hope." Hurtful or discouraging words are simply garbage. We must be diligent in monitoring the words we speak and uprooting from our psyches poisonous words planted there by others.

You can go on to the next chapter if you want to, but now is a good time to stop and schedule some garbage collecting. Let's declare, "Today is garbage day." Go through your heart and mind right now, and see if you can identify any mental or emotional garbage. The de-cluttering, scrubbing agent of *perspective* can work to destroy the negativity that exists if we give it a chance. Let's summarize.

"Putting the lid" on a negative requires specific action—doing something tangible that says, "I've now done all I can do."

Changing our perspective on negatives begins by deciding we want to be positive. This change requires us to look for the good in bad situations and deliberately focus on that good…thinking good thoughts, saying good words, and taking good actions. For perspective to work, we must be persistent in our efforts to "put the lid" on negatives, trumping a negative thought every time it tries to play another card. "Putting the lid" on a negative requires specific action—doing something tangible that says, "I've now done all I can do." Perhaps, that "something" is as small as changing the words we use to discuss the negative. Finally, if the good we seek is not obvious, then, like Elijah, we must keep looking until we find it, believing all the while in our Abiding Good God[17] and His ability to make all things work together for our good.

You're in luck! Here comes the truck! Haul what you've found to the street, and let's move on!

CHAPTER FIVE

Cleaning Agent #2:
Practice the Golden Rule

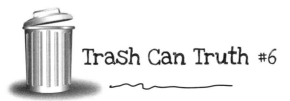

Trash Can Truth #6

Good under-counter, built-in trash compactors have a compression ratio of 5:1.[1]

I've never owned a kitchen trash compactor. The only compactor I use is my foot, pressing down trash in the can to make room for more. I have, though, had the fun of watching a compactor operate.

I was in a friend's kitchen during a Christmas party and watched with amusement as one guest after another opened the trash compactor and tossed in paper plates, cups, plastic forks, food, etc. In time, the compactor was filled to the brim…no room for more trash. Of the several people who were in the kitchen, no one had ever worked this modern convenience.

Assuming my friend's approval, I volunteered to turn

on the compactor. Not knowing exactly what to expect, I pressed the button labeled "ON." Great deduction, don't you think? Within seconds a crunching noise began coming from the machine. Nervous glances ricocheted from one face to the other. We all feared something was wrong, or the racket would summon a concerned host. Thankfully, the noise ceased in a minute or so.

The Golden Rule, as taught by Jesus Christ, is, "Do unto others as you would have them do unto you."

Boldly, I opened the door, and poof, the garbage was gone. Closer inspection revealed that the garbage was not actually gone, but had been pressed far down into the bottom of the compactor, leaving more than 80% of the compactor empty.

After thinking about it, I realized that in human relationships, we have something very similar to a trash compactor for dealing with mental and emotional garbage: The Golden Rule. This age-old philosophy may not eliminate our negative experiences, but it does help minimize them and shrink them to a manageable size.

The Golden Rule, as taught by Jesus Christ, is, "Do unto others as you would have them do to you."[(2)] Christians aren't the only religious people who ascribe to this teaching. Buddha taught his followers, "Hurt not others in ways you yourself would find hurtful."[(3)] When we look in the Islam religion, we find: "No one of you is a believer until he desires for his brother that which he desires for himself."[(4)] And the Hindu followers memorize: "This is the sum of duty; do naught unto others that which would cause you pain if done to you."[(5)] Perhaps, for some, the Golden Rule is more clearly explained in the modern saying, "What goes around, comes around."

The joke is told of the time God and Saint Peter got together and changed the rules for getting into Heaven. No longer was it enough just to believe in Jesus, you had to do something noble with your life. The first person to make it under the new rule was a gynecologist. Saint Peter asked her what noble thing she had done with her life, and she replied she had taken care of women and helped many of them give birth to babies. Saint Peter told her, "That's noble! Come on in!" The second person to make it to Heaven under the new rule was a pediatrician. Saint Peter asked him what noble thing he had done with his life, and he responded he had taken care of boys and girls and helped many of them grow to be healthy adults. Saint Peter said, "That's noble. Come on in." The third person to make it under the new rule was the director of a large Health Maintenance Organization. Saint Peter asked him what noble thing he had done with his life, and he proudly reared back and said, "I was the director of the largest HMO in my state." Saint Peter thought about it for a few minutes and then said, "Okay. You may come on in…but you can only stay three days!"

Literally, what goes around comes around! From any perspective, the Golden Rule is much more than a rule! It's a "law" of human relationships.

Literally, what goes around comes around! From any perspective, the Golden Rule is much more than a rule! It's a "law" of human relationships.

Someone may ask, "How does 'doing for other people the things we want done for us' work to neutralize our negatives?" The answer lies in four truths:

• The Golden Rule activates the "cycle of good."

- The Golden Rule puts me in the driver's seat, empowering me to have control over situations.

- When I give something away, i.e., love, forgiveness, service, I create room to receive something new.

- Getting involved in someone else's problem gets my mind off me and my needs.

Let's take a closer look at each of these.

Trash Can Truth #7

To start the trash compacter,
you must push the "ON" button.

The first reason the Golden Rule works to neutralize negatives is that it activates the "cycle of good." I do a good thing for you; you do a good deed for someone else, and so forth, until the good comes back to me. Think of dominos arranged in a circle, standing on end. If nothing touches them, they remain still…no movement in any direction. However, if something *pushes one of the dominos forward,* that domino will topple onto the second one, etc., until the last standing domino will fall onto the first one. Doing for other people what we would like them to do for us ignites the activity in the circle. The good deed pushes the "ON" button.

A song from the musical *Mary Poppins* is a favorite of mine. The title and repetitive line announce, "A spoonful of sugar makes the medicine go down, in a most delightful way!"[6] Good deeds are sweet to the soul. The more good—or sugar—I can generate during a bad situation, the easier it will be to minimize the garbage and get on with a positive life.

Hurricanes are never any fun, but the "spoonful of sugar," sharing what we had with others, helped the medicine go down...in a most delightful way!

Restoring electricity to the Mississippi Gulf Coast following a hurricane is a Herculean task. I remember an outage that lasted eight days in my neighborhood. By the fourth day, everything in my freezer was thawing. To keep from wasting the frozen beef, chicken, fish, and home-grown vegetables, Dickie fired up the grill in the back yard and invited the neighbors to join us for dinner. They soon contributed their thawing foods.

What a grand party we had, filled with laughter and tall tales. That party lasted on and off for several days until power was restored. We bonded with those neighbors, creating for ourselves newer and richer friendships. Hurricanes are never any fun, but the "spoonful of sugar," sharing what we had with others, helped the medicine go down…in a most delightful way!

The Golden Rule is like the native who tried to throw his old boomerang away—with no success. Each time it came right back to him! Words spoken and deeds performed have that same boomerang effect. When we are in the middle of a bad experience, if we think, say, or do something bad, bad will most likely come back to us. **We cannot plant cactus and expect to harvest apples.** The Holy Bible clearly teaches, "Whatsoever a man sows that shall he also reap."[7]

If we want to start something good coming our way, we must think, say, or do something good for someone else. What we give out *will eventually* come back to us!

The examples are endless. If we want help with a project, we need to help other people with their projects. One of my favorite memories from teaching high school was the French Club tricycle race. Each year, as a fundraiser, the French Club sponsored tricycle races in the gymnasium. The sophomores, juniors, seniors, and faculty all had teams. The race was a relay, with half of each team positioned on both ends of the gym. Grown bodies would ride little tricycles from one end of the gym to the other.

Never once do I remember saying no when asked to participate on the faculty team. Why? Because the French Club sponsor was always so willing to sit as a judge and make suggestions during my play auditions. When plays were presented for the student body, she always encouraged her students to attend and served as a teacher monitor in the auditorium. How could I say no?

I don't remember which one of us started helping the other with projects first. All I know is that my actions always resulted in a reciprocal action. The principle worked not just with the French Club sponsor, but with the band director, football coach, electronics teacher, office secretary—the entire staff! If we want help, we must be helpful.

If we want to have a friend, we must be a friend. We can't rely on one friendly word or action to produce a friend; but, as we persistently send out friendly thoughts, words, and actions toward others, friends will start appearing in our lives. Some of you would probably assume that a person as outgoing and fun-loving as I am would have never had trouble making lots of friends—but you'd be wrong.

When Dickie and I moved to Madison, we didn't know a soul in the town…not one! Oh, we still had plenty of good friends, but they were two and three hours away in other towns. After a few months of not going out to dinner with friends and not sitting in church next to people who knew and loved us, I threw a pity party. I decorated my breakfast table with the Bible, a cup of hot tea, and a washtub for tears. I told God about how sad and lonely I was, and about how nobody cared anything about us here. I begged Him to please give us some good friends. Several weeks went by and my prayer was repeated daily…give us some good friends in this town, though none appeared.

If we want to have a friend, we must be a friend.

Finally, my self-centered will heard the Spirit within me say, "Janie, don't worry about having friends, just be one. Quit thinking about yourself, and start being a friend to others."

No overnight miracles occurred. I didn't twitch my nose and have an instant friend appear. But as I began looking for and seizing opportunities to be a friend, slowly friendships were formed. As new neighbors moved into the neighborhood, I took them casseroles. At Christmastime, Dickie and I invited the other five homes in our cul-de-sac to come over for dinner. We initiated in our Sunday school class rotating supper clubs. Within a year's time, we had eaten lovely meals in almost all of their homes…and more importantly, started the process of making dear friends in Madison.

In "garbage" terms, this forgiveness concept is a big one!

Similarly, if we want to be loved, we must demonstrate our love to others. Once again, consistency wins the day. If I tell you I love you once, you may appreciate the words, but they won't produce love. However, if I tell you often and spend quality time with you and am there for you in your time of need, love will grow between us and come back to me.

If we want to be thanked for what we do, we must thank other people for what they do. Don't just thank people we eventually want something from, but *all* people. Thank the store clerk, postman, janitor, flight attendant, library assistant, online support staff, office receptionist, soldier, teacher, preacher, spouse, and child.

If we want to receive praise for a job well done, we must first do a good job, and then start to praise others for the good work they do. Praise the athlete, soloist, butcher, fisherman, farmer, seamstress, nurse, gardener, and artist.

If we want to be forgiven when we make mistakes, then we must quickly forgive others when they make mistakes. In "garbage" terms, this forgiveness concept is a big one! Everyone wants to be forgiven.

The story is told of a deaf old lady who was faithful to go to confession every Saturday. Because she was deaf, the priest noticed she was hollering her sins all over the cathedral. "Madame," the priest advised, "to keep others from hearing your sins, why don't you write them on a piece of paper and slip them to me under the confessional curtain?" The lady thought that was a grand idea, so the next Saturday she slipped the priest a piece of paper. He said, "Ma'am, I'm a bit confused. This looks like a grocery store list." "Goodness gracious," exclaimed the lady. "I've left my sins at the A&P!"

As funny as this is, wouldn't we all like to leave our "sins" somewhere? Wouldn't we all like to walk away from them and forget they ever happened? Those of us who are Christians know that God forgives us when we repent, and He remembers our sins no more,[8] but people aren't God. We want people to forgive us, too. Anytime we do or say the wrong thing, we want to hear someone respond, "I understand. It's okay. I forgive you." To get forgiveness coming our way, we must be the first to throw the boomerang…start the good effect working…we must forgive others.

Don't wait for good to come your way. Start the cycle of good working. Push the "ON" button.

In short, whatever you find yourself in need of, start doing or saying it to other people. Don't wait for good to come your way. Start the cycle of good working. Push the "ON" button.

Trash Can Truth #8

Garbage is powerless against a trash compactor.

Once the "ON" button of a trash compactor is pushed, the mechanisms inside the machine begin to crush even the biggest boxes and strongest cans. Though the compactor cannot eliminate the garbage, it certainly shrinks the garbage down to size.

Likewise, the second reason the Golden Rule works to minimize garbage is because, like the crushing "mechanism" inside the trash compactor, the Golden Rule gives power to me, putting me in the driver's seat, in a position of control. I'm not just a helpless passenger riding through a bad experience. I have the steering wheel, and I can choose my course of action during the experience.

Thanking, praising, helping, teaching, listening, forgiving are all things I can do…if I want to. The choice is totally mine. The act of giving anything empowers me, and whether or not the recipients want what I give, or feel they deserve it, is not important. If I choose to give something good, I have made a decision and exerted my power.

When we find ourselves in the prison of negativity, one of our most liberating gifts is forgiveness. A young boy was just learning the Lord's Prayer. He got to the passage that says, "And forgive us our trespasses as we forgive those who trespass against us." The word trespass was really big for him. He didn't know how to pronounce it, so he said, "And forgive us our trash baskets as we forgive those who put trash in our baskets."

Now I ask you, what is a trespass but someone trying to put trash in your basket? Empty your basket! Forgive your spouse for nagging and your little leaguer for breaking the window. Forgive your boss for barking at you during stressful deadlines, and forgive drivers for poking along at 40 mph in 55 mph zones. Forgive friends for not including you in luncheons, and forgive neighbors for backing over your tulips. Forgive waiters for bringing salads with the wrong dressing, and forgive pastors for preaching boring sermons.

One lady was new in town and visited a local church. When the service was over, after a particularly long and boring sermon, the lady introduced herself to a gentleman seated near her. "Good morning," she said. "I'm Gladys Dunn." "Good morning," he replied. "I'm glad it's done, too."

The act of giving empowers me, and whether or not the recipients want what I give, or feel they deserve it, is not important.

I've waited impatiently for the end of a few sermons myself, but priests, rabbis, and preachers are only human. What if you had to write two and three speeches per week? Chances are some of them would be yawners, too. Forgive them. Quickly forgiving these little slights is great practice for handling the big garbage in life.

"Trash" often comes in the form of words. The following quotations were reportedly taken from actual federal employee performance evaluations. How would you like it if someone wrote this about you?

• She works well when under constant supervision and cornered like a rat in a trap.

- This young lady has delusions of adequacy.

- He doesn't have ulcers, but he's a carrier.

- When his IQ reaches 50, he should sell.

And one of my favorites:

- The gates are down, the lights are flashing, but the train isn't coming.

When we chose to forgive, whether the other person accepts it or not, we have compacted that trash.

If we harbor negative feelings because of the rude or unkind things people say, those negative feelings become a type of baggage that builds up inside of us, not them. That negative consumes space in our hearts, not theirs. Resentment weighs us down and steals our peace and joy. However, if we want to preserve our peace and joy, we can. The Golden Rule gives us complete control. When we chose to forgive, whether the other person accepts it or not, we have compacted that trash.

We don't forgive people for what it does for them, but because of what forgiving them does for us. Forgiveness rids us of poisonous negative toxins. Never forget, we always have a choice. Are we going to hold on to the negative or let go of it? The Golden Rule puts me in the driver's seat.

Trash Can Truth #9

The average-size kitchen bag of trash contains enough energy to light a 100-watt bulb for more than 24 hours.[9]

The third reason the Golden Rule works to neutralize negatives is that when we give something away, we create more room for new things—perhaps even better things. This principle works in the natural realm, as well as the psychological.

When Dickie and I decided to make the move from Gulfport to Madison, we undertook a massive "de-junking" of our house. We were determined not to move unnecessary tonnage. Our diligent purging produced a huge truckload of stuff that went to Goodwill Industries. Another truck full of junk went to the garbage dump.

The hardest things for me to part with were my clothes. I reasoned, "If they are good enough to give away for someone else to wear, why don't I keep them?!" I'd put a sweater in the bag and then take it out. I'd hold items up and wonder if they would ever come back in style. "If I would just lose ten pounds, these clothes would still work for me," I thought. After many agonizing decisions, I parted with six thirty-gallon garbage bags full of clothes.

Whatever I give away actually makes room for something else— perhaps something even better.

All of that effort was rewarded when we moved into our new house. For the first time in years, I could wear clothes straight from my closet without having to iron them. Dresses were not crammed together. Slacks hung neatly with one inch between each hanger. When I bought new articles of clothing, I had room for them. True, my "heaven" was short-lived because I am who I am, but my joy was great while it lasted! Because I gave something away, I had room for more.

The Golden Rule works the very same way. Whatever

I give away actually makes room for something else—perhaps something even better.

Time is precious to me. For all practical purposes, I'm a one-woman show who runs my own speaking and training business. I'm the secretary, marketing director, research department, product developer, receptionist, travel coordinator, and speaker. When I have a week I'm not pressed into one of those services, I guard it vigilantly.

If we want to eliminate negatives, the gift that is of paramount importance is forgiveness.

One March I found myself with such a week. I looked forward to sleeping late and writing on a new book and shopping, etc. However, the lady who sat with my mother-in-law needed a week off to take care of some business. I heard my mouth saying, "I'll be happy to stay with her while you're gone," but my heart was screaming, "No! I need my week!"

The more I thought about my abandoned plans, the more abused I felt. I dreaded the week. When the time finally came to drive to my mother-in-law's house, I gave myself a good lecture. I loved my mother-in-law. She was sick and needed somebody. I made a conscious decision to "give" her the week. No one was taking the week from me. Nobody was making me do this. I chose to spend the week with her because it was the right thing to do.

Much to my delight, fully equipped with a new attitude, I entered her house that week and had a wonderful time. We cooked, made a pecan pie, watched TV together, and laughed about everything from medicine to milk cows (one of her neighbor's cows strayed into her front yard). What a great week! That was in March. My mother-in-law died in April of congestive heart failure. I will go to my grave ever grateful I gave away a week in order to make room for a lifetime of good memories.

The list of things we can give is endless. We can give love, understanding, time, effort, tolerance, knowledge, acceptance, encouragement…to name only a few. Once again, if we want to eliminate negatives, the gift that is of paramount importance is forgiveness.

Forgiveness works on more levels than just forgiving other people. Sometimes we need to forgive "the system" for overlooking us or allowing us to fall through the cracks. Other times we must forgive ourselves for making mistakes. Plus, **rare occasions actually exist when forgiving God becomes a necessary therapy.**

I remember a specific time when the garbage can of my heart overflowed with trash. A couple of years after we married, Dickie and I decided to start a family. We weren't really sure we wanted a child, but my biological clock was ticking. We needed to start moving in that direction if we were ever going to be parents. My doctor recommended I assist nature by taking some common hormones.

One night, several months into the process, as I lay down to sleep, I was startled to see a huge lump protruding from my abdomen. I quickly asked Dickie if he could see it, too, and he could.

Sleep was difficult that night for both of us. The next morning we began touring doctors. By the next day, I was in the hospital undergoing exploratory surgery.

What the doctor found was a grapefruit-size cyst on my left ovary. Because he knew we were trying to have a child, he only removed the left ovary. However, on the day I was to be dismissed from the hospital, the full lab report came back and indicated cancerous cells in the removed tissue.

The doctor gave me a few choices. He said, "Janie, if cancer is in the left ovary, there's a 25% chance cancer will be in the right one, too. What do you want to do? We can do preventative radiation or chemo therapy on the right ovary, which, by the way, might damage it beyond its ability to produce eggs. If we decide to do nothing, we can check you every three months for five years to make sure there are no changes. Or, we can go back into surgery and remove the right ovary.

Life had thrown me a major curve, and I was mad at God!

The decision really wasn't that hard to make. Though Dickie and I thought we wanted to have a child, we didn't want it badly enough to go through all that treatment uncertainty. The next day I had my second major surgery in eight days, followed by eight long weeks of recovery.

I spent most of that eight weeks pouting and sulking. Even though we weren't passionate about having a child, I didn't want to be told I couldn't have one. To my way of thinking, something was very unfair about all of this. Dickie and I were good people. We were faithful to our church. We kept the Ten Commandments.

Insult was added to injury when I learned three girls in the high school where I taught had abortions that year. God didn't make any sense to me. Why would

He give babies to girls who abort them, and then deny babies to people like us who would love them?

Life had thrown me a major curve, and I was mad at God! The garbage cans in my heart and mind were full to the brim and running over. I wasn't even sure I wanted to believe in God any more. You see, this experience was all about me: what had happened to me; what had been denied me; what was unfair to me.

But, one day....don't you love the conjunction "but?" The word signals a change is on the way. So many of our bad situations need a "but" in them somewhere!

I no longer enjoyed living filled with anger and devoid of faith. Something had to change!

My change came the day I realized I was miserable being mad at God. I had the surgeries to be totally rid of the cancer so I could live. Yet, I no longer enjoyed living filled with anger and devoid of faith. Something had to change!

The first line of the song, "Do-Re-Me," from *The Sound of Music*, is "Let's start at the very beginning— a very good place to start."[10] I took that advice and went all the way back to the beginning of my faith. The "beginning of faith" for me requires just a few simple statements of belief:

- God, the Creator of the universe and all of mankind, is the only God, and He loves me.

- Jesus is His son, who died to save me.

- I accept Jesus as my Savior, and so I confess I am saved, and God is my Father, too.

I decided I didn't have to understand why things happened as they did; I only needed to have faith in God and believe that He was in control. The Bible tells me my faith pleases God,[11] and He will see to it that all things—including barrenness—will work together for my good.[12]

With that new beginning, I officially "forgave" God for all the things I thought He could have prevented, but didn't. I asked Him to forgive me for doubting His love. This act marked the start of my complete healing, and opened the door for God to give me a clear call into public speaking just two weeks later. The Golden Rule once again proved to be a powerful trash compactor! As I gave away forgiveness, I minimized the disappointment and hurt, and made room for a brand-new life.

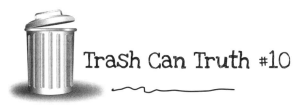

Trash Can Truth #10

I can't smell my garbage when
I'm knee-deep in yours.

The final way the Golden Rule helps us neutralize negatives is by getting our minds off ourselves and focusing them on someone else. The great humanitarian, Albert Schweitzer, once said, "I don't know what your destiny will be, but one thing I know, the only ones among you who will be truly happy, are those who have sought and found how to serve."

Serving others is the perfect way to apply the Golden Rule. We secure happiness for ourselves and neutralize our negatives when we do for other people what we would like for them to do for us.

During my first November in Madison, I was feeling alone and unnecessary. Garbage began to collect in my heart. Donna, a friend who lived in a nearby town, told me of a Thanksgiving project that needed some helping hands. Several hundred pounds of powdered milk, rice, beans, and flour had been donated for the underprivileged families in Jackson. Helpers were needed to divide the food items into family-size plastic bags, to place one of each type into large, brown grocery sacks.

Serving others is the perfect way to apply the Golden Rule.

I agreed to help, and spent a very long evening with dozens of other volunteers from all over the Greater Jackson Area. Not one time did I think about how I felt about life. I was busy helping other people who struggled with bigger "garbage" than I had—finding enough food to eat. My measly problem was nothing time wouldn't heal.

Let's summarize. The Golden Rule is a powerful cleaning agent that teaches us to do for others the things we would like them to do for us. If we practice applying its principle with small trash, we can quickly learn to use it on major, life-altering garbage.

The Golden Rule:

- Begins the cycle of "good" in our lives.

- Gives us power to control negativity.

- Creates room in our lives to receive new and better things.

- Gets our minds off ourselves.

Today is garbage day! Go for the "Gold" by practicing the Golden Rule, and let's start cleaning!

CHAPTER SIX

Cleaning Agent #3:
Maintain Good Self-Esteem

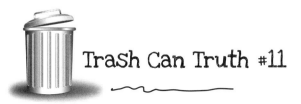

Trash Can Truth #11

Regardless of how I look, I am not garbage.

Gosh! If you could see me in the mornings when I first awake, you wouldn't be reading this book. I'm a sight! My short hair gets pushed upward during the night, with the sides squashed flat and the top electrified. My skin is pale, with pillow marks on my face. I don't look like the well-educated, entertaining, heaven-bound sweet-heart I just know I am. My morning appearance is living proof "we shouldn't judge a book by its cover."

The sad truth is even when I adorn myself as much as possible, I'm still no threat to any runway model. Thank-fully, what I look like is not the equivalent of who I am or how valuable I am. And if you are ever in need of my help, you won't care what I look like!

I remember driving my car late one Halloween night in Atlanta on my way to a speaking engagement. As I rounded a curve on the inside lane of a five-lane road, a tire blew. I temporarily lost control of the car and jumped onto the curb, and then back on the street.

I didn't judge that man by his looks, but by my need. Self-esteem is not about looks!

When I managed to stop the car and observe the damage, I saw the flat tire. Twenty years had passed since I'd last changed a flat, and I'd never done it in the dark. Much to my delight I saw a homeless man walking toward me. He was wearing a long, dirty, beige coat and black gloves, with a ski cap on his head, and carrying a pillowcase-looking sack. As he approached, I called to him, telling him he was an answer to a prayer. God had sent him to my aid.

He offered to change my tire, but when he got on the ground to set the jack, he noticed that not only was my back right tire flat, but my front right tire was flat, as well. Not having two spares, he told me the name of the nearest all-night service station so I could call them to tow the car. By this time, a nice couple stopped to help as well. I paid the man $20, and he went on his way.

The next day when I told my story to the audience, I received nothing but warnings about how dangerous it was for me to trust a homeless man…how I should have just stayed in my car and phoned the police for help. In hindsight, that may have been a safer thing to do, though I'm not sure about sitting in a stopped car in a curve on a dark, busy street. However, that night, I was not seeing in hindsight or foresight. My "right now" sight saw my car broken down on a broad street in Atlanta. My "right now" sight saw not a hobo but a MAN who was capable of changing a tire, and I was willing to pay for his services. I didn't judge that man by his looks, but by my need. Self-esteem is not about looks!

Trash Can Truth #12

Throwing away a garbage can is almost impossible!

My friend John sat at my dining table one night and said in exasperated tones, "Throwing away a garbage can is next to impossible!" He continued to explain how he bought a new can, then set the empty old can on the curb by the full new can, expecting the garbage collectors to see it as garbage, which of course they did not. After turning the old can upside down on one occasion, and on another attempt, precariously trying to prop it against the new can, he finally taped a large poster to the can that read, "I'm throwing this can away. Please take it!"

Like throwing away an old garbage can, disposing

of warped and deflated self-esteem is difficult, too, but not impossible. Self-esteem—the part of my psyche that determines how I feel about myself, how valuable I think others perceive me to be—is a much-talked-about, but little-known, subject.

Often the biggest chunks of garbage that must be destroyed on a regular basis are the negative thoughts and feelings we have about ourselves.

Why even discuss self-esteem in a book designed to help us eliminate the garbage in our lives? The answer: Often the biggest chunks of garbage that must be destroyed on a regular basis are the negative thoughts and feelings we have about ourselves. Some experiences, like divorce, death of a loved one, illness, and unemployment leave us feeling helpless, defenseless, useless…like crumpled trash. Mistakes, failures, accidents, legal difficulties, and conflicts with people all lead us to see ourselves as clumsy, guilty, ignorant, and unworthy. Have I struck a familiar chord with you yet? None of us is perfect.

Trash Can Truth #13

No matter what I've done, I'm not garbage!

Occasionally, I feel stupid and unwanted, when:

- My supervisor berates me and threatens my job.

- I sit at home and no one calls.

- I take a risk—trying to make good things happen—only to be defeated and be worse off than when I started.

Before long, if I don't rise up on the inside and declare otherwise, in my own sight, I will become the biggest piece of garbage in the house!

Most of you know the feeling I'm describing—that sense of being trash, abused by everyone, of no value to anyone, a waste of good air. If you haven't had the "pleasure" of slumming around in Nobodyville lately, please don't go out of your way to visit. Once the human spirit sinks into the valleys of that terrain—also called low self-esteem, the climb back up the mountain to a sense of well-being is often difficult. Some people never make it. Low self-esteem is at the heart of most suicides.

I alone determine if I am indeed valuable to you.

Self-esteem refers specifically to how valuable and worthy I believe myself to be. "Self" is a confusing word when trying to understand this definition. For you see, my value and worth are not about how valuable and worthy I am to myself, but how valuable and worthy I believe myself to be to you! Simply, do I think you need me?

- Do I believe my family, friends, and co-workers need me?

- Do I believe I contribute anything significant to society?

• Do I believe someone would miss me if I died?

Notice the emphasis is on the question, "Do I believe?" What you tell me, or what experience dictates, doesn't matter. The issue is, *"Do I believe I am valuable to the people in my life?"* I alone determine if I am indeed valuable to you.

For 29 years, I taught school at the secondary and college levels. Some of those mornings, I awoke sick or exhausted. Everything in me screamed, "Go back to sleep!" With few exceptions, however, I would get dressed, go to school, and teach all day. Why? Because I believed those students needed me and the instruction I could give them more than they needed a substitute teacher. I believed I was valuable to them. This created self-esteem.

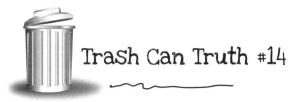

Trash Can Truth #14

The more you kick a can, the sooner your shoes will be garbage!

Low self-esteem often produces its kissin' cousin—low self-worth. "I'm not worthy" or "I don't deserve" are two mentalities we all encounter periodically. During Christmas one year, I felt achy all over. Between working, cooking, shopping, cleaning, and decorating, I had become stressed and grumpy. I knew a couple of hours (yes, hours) on a massage table listening to soothing music would make a world of difference to my body, but it was Christmas. The economy was bad—a time when people should think of buying for others, not themselves. For several days I deliberated, finally deciding to give myself a Christmas present. I almost missed a healing experience for my body and soul because I felt it was too much money to spend on myself.

Self-worth is not only about how worthy I feel of tangible things I like massages, but also how worthy I feel myself to be of your help, your attention, your love and friendship, your involvement in my life. **The friends we have say far more about what we think of ourselves than what we think of them.** Sometimes we won't even try to be friends with certain people because we think, "They won't like me. They're so important, and I'm a nobody."

Our inability to ask for help is a prime example of low self-worth.

Our inability to ask for help is a prime example of low self-worth. We may not feel worthy of help. I taught across the hall from a teacher who struggled with computers. Our school installed a new computer program and hired someone to be on staff to answer our questions as we learned the applications. When I ran into trouble with the program, I phoned the staff member so much, he recognized my voice by just hearing, "Hello!"

One day I saw my teacher friend banging his head

with his hands. When I went to see if I could help, I found his computer was not responding to any commands, and I had no idea how to correct it. I asked if he had called the staff member and he said no; he hated to bother him. *Bother him?*, I thought. *It's his job! That's why he was hired—to help us.* The lack of self-worth had struck again. Think of the mental and emotional garbage my friend generated while struggling with the computer…needing help, but not wanting to bother anyone for it! Needless to say, we quickly got the help we needed, and both of us went back to work.

I can't point a finger at anyone without pointing three back at me. We've all had times when our self-esteem was low, when we felt no one really needed us or wanted us—times when we thought we didn't deserve good things. Those times usually come on the heels of some other type of garbage—sickness, failure, arguments, defeat, thoughtless comments, loss of control…you name it.

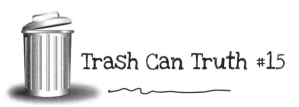

Trash Can Truth #15

The first-known landfill was developed for refuse in Knossos, Crete, in 1500 BC.[1]

In spite of their ingenious solution to the garbage problem, the architects of Crete only managed to cover up the problem. For centuries, we have followed their example and simply buried our garbage. This has led to the formation of toxic fumes called methane gas. But modern science has discovered a way to use this toxic gas to generate electricity for powering industrial facilities that provide lighting and temperature control to homes and businesses, or for using as fuel for our vehicles.[2] What if we were to do the same with our negativity, transforming low self-esteem and low self-worth into productive energy? Thankfully, converting this garbage simply requires us to use the replacement technique: replace bad thoughts and feelings with good thoughts and feelings. How is that done? The answer to that question is found in three categories:

- Exercising faith in God.

- Developing positive relationships.

- Producing meaningful accomplishments.

For a Christian, the Bible and our faith in God are critical to self-esteem. The Holy Spirit tells us that God so loved the people of the world that He sent His only Son Jesus to the earth to live and die for us. If anyone would believe in Jesus and accept Him as Savior, that person would have everlasting life.[3] Think of that! The God who created the universe and breathed life into human beings, loved you and me so much that He sent His only Son Jesus to pay the ultimate price for all of our sins and wrongdoings, a.k.a. garbage. Jesus washed us clean with His blood and made us "right" in God's sight just so we could live eternally with God.

In return for this promise of everlasting life, God asks us to love Him[4] and to serve Him[5]. Meditate on that! ***The God of the universe needs us to do His work on the earth. God loves us, and He needs us!*** He paid a high price for us. He thinks we are worthy of all the great things He has planned for us!

**Dear friend, I can tell you
God loves you, but until you decide
to believe it for yourself,
self-esteem will be a struggle.**

The Bible goes on to tell us God cares so much for us, He has the very hairs of our head numbered.[6] Every tear we've ever shed, He's collected in a jar;[7] He's got a plan for our lives that is good, and promises a hope and a future;[8] He will be with us always—even until the end of the world;[9] and, He's got a mansion prepared for us, just waiting for our arrival in Heaven![10] Wow! If we can ever get to the point that we really believe all the promises we read in the Bible about God's love for us, self-esteem would be a cinch! Dear friend, I can tell you God loves you, but until you decide to believe it for yourself, self-esteem will be a struggle.

Developing positive relationships is also critical to possessing good self-esteem. Abraham Maslow, in his Hierarchy of Human Need theory, listed self-esteem as one of the most important needs in human beings.

Maslow defined self-esteem as having the respect of your peers—or in the language of this book—maintaining good relationships with the people in your life. He argued that without self-esteem, we could not reach our maximum potential for personal growth and fulfillment.[11]

Relationships are built by:

- Sharing each others' thoughts and dreams.

- Being there when people need us.

- Keeping in touch through phone calls, emails, visits, and letters.

- Sharing meals together.

- Giving gifts.

- Not saying everything you think.

- Saying important things people need to hear.

- Speaking the truth in love.

- Believing the best about people.

- Forgiving mistakes, even when mistakes hurt you.

- Participating in activities together.

- Working on goals together.

- Being a cheerleader.

- Loving people even if they don't yet love you.

- Praying for people.

In short, if you think something will help a person, do it. If you think it will hurt them unnecessarily, don't do it. Follow that simple principle, and you will have good relationships. Keep at your efforts until a deep and lasting relationship forms. Know in your heart that the relationship matters to you and that you matter to the other person. When you reach that point, the point where you know that you matter to the other person, self-esteem is yours!

In short, if you think something will help a person, do it.

Strive to have good relationships with your family, friends, neighbors, church leaders, employers, co-workers, clients, service providers, and anyone else who moves into your sphere of influence. In the mix, don't forget to form a good relationship with yourself!

All the things listed before to do for others, do the same for you, too. Decide to like yourself, and value the time spent alone with just you. A line from the prose poem, *Desiderata*, written by Max Ehrmann, says, "You are a child of the universe, no less than the trees and the stars. You have a right to be here!"[12]

You don't have to be wealthy, well-known, or influential to have good self-esteem.

Even hobos can have good self-esteem. The story is told of a wealthy elderly lady who was disgruntled by the sight of a ragged hobo. "You filthy man," she exclaimed. "Don't you even have a handkerchief?" "Yeah, I do, lady," the hobo replied, "but I don't like loanin' it to just anybody."

I repeat, you don't have to be wealthy, well-known, or influential to have good self-esteem. You just have to be a person who is willing to enter into relationships and believe those people need you.

When Dickie died, I struggled with self-esteem on this very issue. I knew down deep in my "knower" that Dickie needed me when he was alive. With him gone, I didn't think anyone needed me. One of my most pitiful laments was, "The only two creatures on the planet whose lives would be changed if I didn't exist are my two

Italian Greyhounds, Winston and Venice." Family and friends tried to tell me otherwise saying, "Janie, we'd miss you." I countered by saying, "Your life wouldn't change in any way if I weren't here. You don't really need me!"

Finally, "the teacher" remembered the concept she taught others—what people tell you about you is not as important as what you believe about yourself. People can tell me I matter to them, but if I don't believe I matter to them, then their words won't matter! (Ha!)

Trash Can Truth #16

It takes 550 years for disposable diapers to decompose, and more than one million years for Styrofoam to decompose![13]

Thankfully, low self-esteem doesn't take years to "decompose." We can start today believing we are needed by the people in our lives. All it takes are a few, positive actions.

- Stop saying you're not needed. Remember, garbage out—garbage in.

- **Stop thinking negative thoughts about your life. Your mind is *your* mind. You can think anything you want to think. Choose positive thoughts on purpose—in spite of how you feel!**

- Tell people how much they mean to you. Tell your postal workers, garbage collectors, primary physicians, religious staff, neighbors, friends, family, and God. Magnify these relationships in your mind.

- Deliberately do good deeds for people. In particular, look for people who have a need, then fill that need.

- Stop thinking about yourself so much. Think of others. Think about the beauty of sunsets and the sweet smell of roses.

- Throw yourself into activities and projects that are fun and beneficial. Idol hands and minds are most certainly the devil's workshop.

Continue to repeat these steps until you know for sure the people in your world are better off because you live in it.

The third category in which self-esteem grows is the area of accomplishments—do I believe I've accomplished anything that makes me valuable to you or worthy of your respect?

We evaluate our accomplishments by asking questions like:

- *What have I done to make my world a better place*—pick up trash, give to a worthy cause, vote for an honest candidate?

- *What do I offer that makes a difference in people's lives*—help with projects, support during a crisis, dinner at my home?

- *When I put my head on the pillow at night and look back over my day, what deeds make me feel proud of the way I lived that day*—notes to a shut-in, flowers planted in a garden, groceries carried to a car for an elderly lady?

- *Have I done anything that improved my lot in life*—read a good book, contacted a client, learned a new word, exercised?

- *What obstacles have I overcome*—balanced a checkbook, apologized to a friend, made time to visit a new neighbor?

- *What challenges have I successfully met and conquere*d—located an online source for a hard-to-find item, mastered a computer function, cleaned a closet?

- *What temptation did I rise above*—passed on dessert at lunch, refused to listen to office gossip, turned off the TV reruns?

Much in literature talks about "a life well spent." That phrase implies we actually exchange the hours of our lives for some activity. Poets also write mournfully about "the wasted life." That phrase implies our choices of activities are sometimes poor—we had great potential but did not develop the potential well. Looking back over what we believe to be a wasted hour—a wasted life—creates low self-esteem.

Worthwhile accomplishments come in all sizes, large and small. Some occur in a short amount of time, and others over years. I received a phone call from a dear friend early one Saturday morning. (I don't do early often, and rarely on Saturday mornings!) She and her husband had just placed their last house note in the mail. They now owned their house!

**Worthwhile accomplishments come in all sizes, large and small.
Some occur in a short amount of time, and others over years.**

I could tell by her voice she was beaming. The purchase had been a fifteen-year commitment—a time period that included sending two daughters to college for bachelors' and masters' degrees, weddings for both daughters, a job change with decrease in pay for her, and a nine-month period when her husband had no job. In spite of the difficulties, their efforts had prevailed. They owned a beautiful home—a major life accomplishment! She had a right to be proud. Her self-esteem was high!

Another friend hammered the last nail into a family room he was adding onto his house. He had done almost all of the work himself, saving hundreds of dollars in labor costs. His self-esteem was high!

Saving a child from drowning, graduating from school, learning a new language—these are just a few examples of major accomplishments that can build good self-esteem in us. However, good self-esteem is also built by the thousands of small deeds we do, often without even thinking about them.

My eyes are drawn to beautiful jewelry. Because I appreciate compliments on jewelry I wear, I've made it a habit to compliment others. I say, "That's gorgeous (or unique, delicate, eye catching, stunning…you get the idea?)!" When I notice a diamond-studded wedding ring, I add, "Somebody must really love you!" Those simple words—said so many times now I don't even think about them—have made me the recipient of heart-touching stories. I hear about the memorable trip, or cherished grandmother, or determination it took to save the money. In return, my self-esteem gets a booster shot! I've given a person a chance to shine! Such a little thing for so many good feelings!

Small accomplishments! I passed a lady in an airport bathroom that appeared to be looking for something on the floor. I stopped and inquired. She said she had dropped an earring. Just like you would have done, I began to help her look for it. Soon, others joined the search, and before long the missing earring was found. The lady was so appreciative. She said thank you, not once, but several times. That good deed cost me less than two minutes, but I knew it had made a difference in that woman's life, so I felt good about me. I wasn't even the lady who found the earring, but I was a part of the search!

Believe in the wealth of good you have to offer your world.

My husband never passed a beggar on the street without putting change in his bucket. The amount was not always a lot—fifty cents here, five dollars there, sometimes more. When he had no change, I've actually seen him go get change, and bring it back for the bucket. Dickie knew the arguments about how the money is wasted on booze and drugs, but he rarely felt "taken to the cleaners" by the less fortunate. On the contrary, the sight of them made Dickie realize his blessings. He understood he couldn't eradicate all the problems, but he wanted to do the little bit he could to help. The beggar was better off, and so was Dickie's self-esteem.

Self-esteem is a powerful cleaning agent that makes our minds and hearts stain-resistant!

In summary, let's get busy gathering all the negative experiences, unkind words, and self-defeating thoughts that dare attack us at the very core of our being…causing us to doubt our value and minimize our importance to God and the people in our world. **Bag that trash and haul it to the street!** Don't stop, however, with that action. Get to work on your faith. **You are alive because God wants you to be alive. The God who created the universe needs you!** Work, also, on building strong relationships and striving for worthwhile accomplishments. Believe in yourself. Believe in the wealth of good you have to offer your world.

Self-esteem is a powerful cleaning agent that makes our minds and hearts stain-resistant! The stronger our self-esteem, the less garbage we'll accumulate. Hurry! Today is garbage day!

CHAPTER SEVEN

Cleaning Agent #4:
Laugh!

Trash Can Truth #17

Garbage cans eventually get dirty!

After months of taking out the garbage, even the most meticulous will find themselves with dirty garbage cans. Liquids have leaked from bags, and odors have permeated its walls. The can itself—devoid of any garbage—begins to reek. Water alone is powerless against the stench and stains. A strong cleaning agent is needed.

Likewise, our hearts and minds, which serve as internal garbage receptacles for life's external trash, will become stained and soiled over time. In the past, we've managed to eliminate much of the garbage, though some has oozed into our subconscious. The smell from that hidden garbage eventually makes its way to the surface. That odorous residue begins to subtly affect our thoughts and behaviors. We become cynical, distrusting, irritable, unhappy, and, in general, dissatisfied with life. Laughter to the rescue! Read on as I reveal laughter's amazing cleaning capacities.

King Solomon, one of the wisest men who ever lived, as recorded in the bestselling book of all times—the Holy Bible—said, "A merry heart doeth good like a medicine, but a broken spirit drieth the bones."[1] Many Americans suffer from "dry bones"…literally!

A merry heart doeth good like a medicine, but a broken spirit drieth the bones. —Proverbs 17:22

Arthritis and osteoporosis are prevalent conditions. Research has linked these and numerous other diseases to stress, which in large part is nothing more than an accumulation of negative garbage. Fortunately, research has also determined laughter benefits our bones, serving as an internal gymnasium, helping bones and joints to absorb calcium and stay lubricated and flexible.

Laughter does far more for our bodies than help our bones. Many of the negatives in life we encounter are due to sickness—colds, flu, insomnia, headaches, immune deficiencies, hormone imbalances, high blood pressure, heart disease, cancer, diabetes. Need I go on? Good news! Laughter has proven to be a valuable ally in dealing with all of these illnesses.

Laughter stimulates the production of endorphins, which is the body's own natural morphine. Do you have a sickness that causes physical pain? If yes, laugh! Give yourself a shot of pain-killing morphine!

Laughter stimulates the production of endorphins, which is the body's own natural morphine.

I've seen laughter work to reduce pain dozens of times. My mother, who lived with me the last five years of her life, suffered with arthritis. I can remember days I'd come home from work, go to my mother's room, and hear about the pains of the day. When my turn came to talk, I would tell Mom about all the crazy speeches I'd heard that day, and the funny things students said. I engaged her mind in things other than sickness. Before long, she'd laugh. Frowns would give way to smiles, and pain would not be mentioned.

Laughter also stimulates the production of antibodies

and killer T-cells. Are you fighting a disease? **Laugh, and laugh often.** Every laugh will produce disease-fighting weapons in your body.

Dr. Norman Cousins, in his book, *The Anatomy of an Illness*, explains clearly how this principle worked in his life. He was suffering from a connective tissue disease, which was very painful and, eventually, could be deadly. His doctors told him he had two choices:

- He could stay on the pain medication and die a relatively painless death.

- He could get off the pain medication (which was preventing the production of antibodies) and give his body a chance to heal itself.

Dr. Cousins researched his options, and in doing so, found a laughter study conducted in the 1940s. One of the conclusions of the study was that laughter reduced pain. Based on those findings, Dr. Cousins chose option number two. He stopped taking pain medication and required everyone who visited him to come with a joke or something funny. He watched a steady diet of silly sitcoms, and even if the episodes weren't fall-out-of-your-chair funny, he responded with hearty belly laughs to each scene.[2]

What was the result of this unorthodox approach

to fighting pain and sickness? The disease died, and Dr. Cousins lived! Laughter is a win-win gift any way you look at it. Had the story ended differently—he laughed and laughed and then died—I contend he would have still succeeded by really living his last days. He wouldn't have spent them fearful and depressed, dreading death, but hopeful and happy, enjoying life. What a way to go!

Even if you're not fighting a disease, the antibodies that laughter produces will strengthen the immune system and ward off disease. Plus, the antibodies flood your system with a wonderful feeling of health! Happiness is easier to achieve in a healthy body, though admittedly, not guaranteed.

Trash Can Truth #18

To clean a dirty garbage can, squirt some dishwashing liquid in the bottom of your empty can, and use a sprayer attachment to a garden hose to "pressure wash" the inside of the offensive smelling can.

The vast majority of the negatives in our lives are not physical, but mental and emotional.

- Worry tops the list. We worry about everything from babies to bank balances, governments to golf games, and Aunt Agnes to Al-Qaeda.

- Hurry is another thief of our peace as we rush to work, rush to church, and rush to meetings. We quickly swallow a meal so we can dash to something fun, or something more important, or just something else! Our vocabularies are filled with the words, "I have to…" or "I must…" instead of "I want to…" or "I will…."

• Relationships and all the stresses created by dealing with people—family, friends, and total strangers—add to the mountain of garbage!

• Factor in all of life's little disappointments over which we have no control: your college football team loses to an instate rival; your neighbor's dog barks late into the night; the stock market takes an unexpected plunge; or your daughter's outdoor wedding is spoiled by rain.

• Finally, let's not forget those national political elections that drive even the stoutest of citizens to their knees pleading for God's mercy!

How can we successfully handle *all* of this garbage?

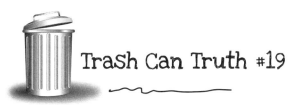

Trash Can Truth #19

Chicken skins are best left in freezers until garbage day!

We've gone through all the right motions to collect the garbage, bag it, stuff it in the can, and put a lid on it, hoping we've camouflaged the sight and odor until the garbage collectors make their way to our house. Unfortunately, like decaying chicken skins, some odors are too strong for the can!

The real life application of this concept is easy. For example, we've systematically moved through all the known steps of grieving over the death of someone dear, the loss of a job, a divorce, or one of the many other awful things that can occur. Having done that, we're now going through the motions of getting on with our lives; but, the repugnant smell of the experience defies our efforts to conceal it. Disappointment, regret, resentment, uncertainty, all betray us. The odor emerging from our spirits is slight, but detectable to the observant.

Our bodies and souls, like dirty trash cans, need a good scrubbing with a powerful cleaning agent —a.k.a. laughter!

You ask, "What becomes of this residue, Janie— these clinging memories that won't let go? After all, we've done what you suggested. We've changed our perspective and practiced the Golden Rule. We've kept a good grip on our value as human beings, all of which you've recommended. We've collected the garbage, put it by the street, and returned the empty cans to the garage, but the smell from yesterday lingers. What are we to do now?"

The answer is laugh! Our bodies and souls, like dirty trash cans, need a good scrubbing with a powerful cleaning agent—a.k.a. laughter! At some point we must come to grips with the fact that no matter how hard we try, we cannot baptize cats! We cannot wear polka-dotted underwear under white shorts, and we can't trust dogs to watch our food. The Bible teaches, "Having done all, stand."[3] When we've done all we can do to eliminate or minimize the negative, stand and just laugh. Scrub the subconscious with our sense of humor.

"Humor?" you ask. "How can that help? Our situation is dull to dilapidated. Living, and the stresses it produces, has hardened our arteries and squeezed the very life out of our cardiovascular systems. Our vision is blurred to the beauty around us, and we're deaf to the rhythm of life that produces peace. We're a modern mess. We're smiling on the outside and disappointed with the hand life has dealt us on the inside. How can humor help?"

Ta-da!!!!!

Humor comes from the Latin word *umor,* which means fluid, **like water. Humorous thoughts, laughter, or even that enlightened smile on your face, is the fluid inside us that washes us clean!** The internal jogging of laughter swishes this fluid around in our hearts and minds and scrubs on our emotions to remove the stains and odors.

A sense of humor, according to C.W. Metcalf and

Roma Felible in their book *Lighten Up*, is a "set of survival skills that keeps us fluid and flexible instead of allowing us to become rigid and breakable."[4] Having a sense of humor doesn't mean you're a stand-up comedian. I'm not suggesting that you go around spouting puns or playing practical jokes—laughing at someone else's expense. Using your sense of humor just means you act and react with lightness. Like Metcalf and Felible suggest, you lighten up!

Having a sense of humor doesn't mean you're a stand-up comedian . . . Using your sense of humor just means you act and react with lightness.

We all know people who are the life of the party as long as everything is going well. These people laugh boisterously. However, when the going gets tough and life deals them a blow, they become mean and vengeful. What we have in that person is not someone with a good sense of humor. We have instead a person who is smart enough to recognize a punch line, but not strong enough to take a punch.

Punches are inevitable. Even an infant knows life is

filled with punches. What baby loves wet diapers, colicky stomachs, or loud, strange noises? None I know. As we grow, the size of life's punches seems to grow with us. All the "D" words attack—death, disease, disappointment, defeat, discouragement, demotion, departure, disgruntled, demanding, dysfunctional—to name only a few.

A sense of humor to the rescue! The story is told of a strong, muscular woman who went to the docks at the Port of Houston to get a job. She was determined that being a woman wasn't going to keep her from doing "man's work." To humor her, they gave her a job unloading cargo from the ships to the dock. The first shipment to arrive was a load of heavy, cast-iron, blacksmith anvils. It didn't help that the forklift was broken, but she was determined to prove she could do the job. She rolled up her sleeves and began carrying the heavy anvils from the ship, across the plank, to the dock.

On one of her trips across the plank, the plank broke! She fell into the water. She went under the first time. She struggled to the surface and then went under a second time. Just before she went under the third time she hollered, "If someone doesn't help me, I'm going to drop one of these anvils!"

"What a nut," we exclaim! However, just like this

woman, some of us are going down for the second and third times. We've already forgiven the offense, we've overlooked that unkind remark, we've rolled with the unexpected punch, and we've regained our balance after life's harsh realities knocked us off our feet. Though we've eliminated most of the garbage, the bag leaked! The stain remains. What now? Laugh! Laughter is a natural cleaning fluid for the soul.

Even though laughter is a natural response, we often need to be reminded to laugh. Why? One reason is we're too diversified…we're doing too much. Like the clown in the circus juggling his bowling pins, as long as he only has four or five pins in the air, he's laughing and joking with the kids on the front row. However, when he adds that sixth and seventh bowling pin, his eyes are permanently fixed on them, knowing if he drops one, he could get clobbered.

Think of all the bowling pins we have in the air! Most of us have jobs outside our homes. We're good workers, so we get to work early and often stay late. Because of that, we're like the farmer who complained to the stranger passing by, saying, "Young man, I work sixteen hours a day, seven days a week." The stranger asked him, "What do you grow?" The farmer replied, "I grow very tired." We grow very tired, too, and that exhaustion often leads to negative experiences and emotions.

Work is not the only bowling pin we have in the air! We have families who deserve and demand our time and attention. When I ask audiences what is a source of stress for them, "Children! Spouses! Parents! Relatives!" are some of the first words spoken. Families—it's hard to live with them, but we can't imagine living without them! Want to wash away some of the stains left by family members? Laugh!

Though we've eliminated most of the garbage, the bag leaked! The stain remains. What now? Laugh!

I asked one teacher friend who had seven children, "How in the world do you get all seven of your children's attention at one time?" She said, "Janie, it's easy. I just sit down and look comfortable!"

Marriage is a challenge, too. I've heard it said, "When a newly married couple smiles, everyone knows why. When a couple that's been married for twenty years smiles, everyone wonders why!" Really! You know the honeymoon is over when the husband calls home to say he'll be late for dinner and the answering machine says, "Dinner is in the microwave."

Work and families are not the only responsibilities keeping us from fun in times of stress. Our activities include civic clubs, youth sporting leagues, tennis teams, garden clubs, political campaigning, and church…let's not forget our churches.

Even though we regularly take out the garbage, the smell in the can intensifies.

Churches will have you teaching Sunday school, singing in the choir, serving on the hospitality committee, going on mission trips, and more. I asked a friend of mine if she'd like to join my church, and she said, "Janie, I'd love to, but I'm not physically able!"

Did you follow all of that? Though a sense of humor is a natural part of our psychological makeup, the responsibilities of work, families, church meetings, and civic commitments distract us. We forget to laugh. We forget to look on the bright side—to search for the silver lining. With our eyes diligently focused on our problems and responsibilities, even though we go through all the motions of regularly taking out the garbage, the smell in the can intensifies.

Do you need a good laugh? Bob Levy, a metro columnist for the *Washington Post* collects funny T-shirt slogans from his readers. See if you can get a chuckle from one of these:

- God made us sisters…Prozac made us friends.

- My mother is a travel agent for guilt trips.

- A princess, having had sufficient experience with a prince, seeks a frog.

- Seen on the back of a passing motorcyclist: "If you can read this, my wife fell off."

- If you want breakfast in bed, sleep in the kitchen.

- If at first you don't succeed, skydiving isn't for you.

And my personal favorite:

- What if the hokey pokey really *is* what it's all about?!

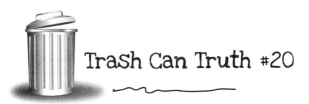

Trash Can Truth #20

87% of Americans have access to curbside or drop-off paper recycling programs.[5]

Eighty-seven is an impressive percentage for having access to paper recycling, but our access to humor weighs in at a perfect 100%! Anyone can laugh anytime and anywhere. Plus, the health benefits ascribed to laughter are mounting. Though research and documentation exists to prove each one, let me simply list a few of the benefits for you.

Laughter has been proven to:

• Diminish physical pain.

• Improve job satisfaction.

• Increase worker productivity.

- Strengthen the heart muscle.

- Lower blood pressure.

- Stimulate creativity.

- Reduce stress.

- Build the immune system.

- Help prevent colds and sore throats.

- Enhance information retention.

- Promote mental flexibility.

All of these benefits would be enough to justify the need to laugh regularly, but the pie gets even sweeter. **Laughter fosters a constructive attitude toward mistakes and elevates our mood.** Who among us hasn't felt the pangs of regret over mistakes? I've heard about the man who said, "I've only been wrong once in my life. Yeah. I thought I made a mistake, but I was wrong." Like I said, I've heard about him, but I've never met him.

Most of us have made more mistakes than we care to remember. I've lost important items, wrecked cars, forgotten deadlines, said unkind words, exercised poor judgment in people, been disrespectful to parents, and flat-out sinned…to name only a few! What garbage!

As awful as these things are, other people have experienced mistakes with even greater consequences. Some of our mistakes result in the deaths of people we love. Some mistakes betray our spouses and destroy our homes. Others ruin our reputations and land us in prison for a lifetime. Only heaven knows all the dreadful things many innocent, God-fearing people do simply by mistake.

Regardless of what the mistake is, responsible people go through the same steps to right a wrong: we dutifully ask for forgiveness, admit to any wrongdoing, and correct the mistakes when possible. Sometimes we can. Sometimes we can't. However, even if we're successful in correcting the mistake, the memory of it can leave a stain that taunts us for years. What are we to do? Laughter comes once again to the rescue. Apply laughter generously, and watch that stain fade!

Especially when we've made a bad mistake, if we can ever get to the point where we can laugh again, we can diminish the ever-accusing memory. Don't get me wrong. We never want to laugh about hurting someone or destroying something important. That's not what it means to laugh following a mistake. Our number one goal is simply to be able to laugh again—to get to the place where sorrow, guilt, and regret can be trumped by peace and happiness found in everyday activities! We want to sincerely pray like David, who committed adultery and had a man killed: "Restore unto me the joy of my salvation."[6] One of God's medicines used in restoring joy is laughter—a merry heart!

Apply laughter generously, and watch that stain fade!

Mistakes are never wasted on me. I always find a way to work them into a speech. Remarkably, most of the time when I tell an audience about some terrible thing I've done, they laugh! Like the time I told the audience about running into a large black cow on a blacktop road in the black of night. The event was traumatic to me. I told the audience how I phoned my husband, and I recited to them his reply. After he asked about my well-being, if I needed him to come to me, the health of the cow, and the condition of our car, he paused and asked incredulously, "Janie, you couldn't see a cow in the middle of the road?!"

The audience roared! Strangely enough, when they laughed, I did, too. After all, I was not harmed and neither was the cow. The cow was so big I only knocked him off his feet. He walked away from the experience, leaving me with a broken headlight and a huge dent on my hood…both of which were repaired.

I could have developed a phobia about night driving, believing myself to be a dangerous driver, but I didn't. Instead, I started laughing at myself. No, I'm not happy I hit a cow. No, I'm not happy my insurance had the expense of fixing my car, or that Dickie and I had to pay the deductible. Yes, I am happy to admit to you I am a fully grown human being who makes mistakes. I am not perfect, nor will I ever be! **As long as I can laugh, I can feel and experience humanity at its best, in spite of mistakes.**

Trash Can Truth #21

Owners often avoid placing really dirty garbage in newly cleaned cans.

Laughter not only rids us of the stain and smell of our negative, it attracts joy. People like to be around a happy, laughing person. Companies want to hire cheerful employees.

I like the story a doctor once told. He was called to deliver a baby at a cabin deep in the woods. The expectant couple had no car, no running water, and no electricity. When the doctor finally found the house, the husband was a nervous wreck. To calm him and to give him something specific to do, the doctor handed the husband a lantern and told him to hold it up high so the doctor could see.

In just a few minutes, the baby was born. As the doctor cleaned the baby and handed it to the mother, the husband started to lower the lantern so he could hold the baby, too, but the doctor said, "Wait. I think there's another baby coming." Up went the lantern and sure enough, out came another baby.

Following the same procedure, the doctor cleaned this second baby, handed it to the mother, and the husband started to lower the lantern, so he could hold one of his children. Then, the doctor said in astonishment, "This is incredible. Get that lantern back up there. I think there's going to be another baby."

The stunned father stood frozen for a moment then asked, "Doc, do you think maybe it's the light that's attracting them?"

Unlike babies, we don't care how many laughs we attract. The more the merrier. **Hold up a light! Search for the bright and funny side of dark experiences.** Laugh. If you're being weighed down by mental and emotional garbage, take a big dose of laughter. Apply this cleaning tool, and scrub away! Don't wait for something to be funny. Just laugh. The physical act of laughing is what gives us the benefits.

To add more laughter to your life, get around people who laugh. Read funny books, watch television sitcoms, or go to funny movies. Buy funny tapes, or collect cartoons and funny posters. Go to dinner with friends, or call a friend and share a joke. Take a fun vacation, play a game with children, or plan a party for work. Just laugh! Develop your sense of humor.

If you're being weighed down by mental and emotional garbage, take a big dose of laughter.

Fun is a tiny word. If we don't guard it carefully, it will get lost among the big and important sounding words like investments, protocol, expenses, and accountability. Squeeze fun into those big words. For after all, fun is **fun**da**mental** to good mental and emotional health.

CHAPTER EIGHT

Cleaning Agent #5:
Assume Responsibility for Your Feelings!

Trash Can Truth #22

We must assume responsibility
for our own garbage.

When my garbage cans are full and need to be hauled to the street, it is my responsibility to do the hauling or see to its doing. I don't expect my neighbors to do it for me. Likewise, we own, and are responsible for, our mental and emotional garbage. **The task of keeping me mentally and emotionally healthy belongs to me and no one else!**

The following garbage story comes from an experience not unfamiliar to some of you. The Christmas Day meal and gift-giving were over. The guests had gone home. All of the wrappings, packaging, turkey bones and other garbage had accumulated to a larger-than-usual amount. Lucky for us, Christmas had been on Monday, and regular garbage pick-up would resume on Tuesday, so off to the street we went with our trash.

I knew it wasn't totally wise to leave the lids propped precariously on top of the overflowing cans; however, I thought the weight of the lids might keep the wind from blowing things around…and it was late…and the garbage trucks always came early, so we left the garbage on the street at midnight and went to bed, thrilled at the triumph of a clean house so quickly.

As much as I'd wanted to turn away from the mess and walk back inside, the trash was mine.

When morning came…surprise! I awoke to a southern-style white Christmas. No, snow had not fallen during the night. Instead, our yard was covered with those annoying white Styrofoam peanuts and white tissue paper, plus bows, bottles, and boxes of all descriptions.

I deduced the turkey bones buried in the bottom of the can still smelled like a good meal to the nearby animals. As much as I wished it hadn't happened, and as much as I'd wanted to turn my face away from the mess and walk back inside, the trash was mine. The cleaning job was my responsibility.

I was tempted to play the blame game, but experience has taught me blaming is a waste of energy. I could have stood in my yard that morning and said, "This is not my fault. I left that garbage neatly stacked. The neighborhood dogs caused this mess. Their owners should clean this." I could have complained about the weather, accusing the wind of spreading the debris. The only problem with either one of these complaints was, after getting myself all riled up, I would still have a yard to clean.

Like this Christmas garbage, the garbage that clutters our hearts and minds is generated by numerous sources—some insignificant, some powerful. **The blame game could be endless. Do we really want to play it?**

Making people or things responsible for our unhappiness could produce mountains of heartbreaking garbage. We could spend the rest of our lives pointing accusing fingers.

In spite of this, if you still want to play the blame game, then let's start by blaming nature. Nature creates devastating garbage with tornadoes, hurricanes, fires, floods, ice storms, mudslides, droughts, and earthquakes. Add to nature's harms the diseases that attack our bodies, and accidents that lurk behind every morning's sunrise.

If we're hurting, other people are surely to blame. Let's blame our spouses, children, parents, siblings, relatives, neighbors, friends, teachers, preachers, authorities, governmental leaders, enemies abroad, and even the devil!

While we're blaming, let's not forget God. Surely with all of His power and foreknowledge, He could have prevented some of this garbage. Let's blame God. Go ahead. Become bitter and curse the day you were born. Keep on until you've generated a heart full of garbage, one overflowing with ugliness. Feel better? Of course not! You feel awful!

I hope you're saying, "Okay, Janie, you've convinced me. I won't play the blame game; but I've got such a mess in my heart. How do I clean this garbage? Where do I start?" You clean your mess the same way I cleaned my yard. I didn't blame anybody or anything—not even myself. I saw the mess, knew it belonged to me, and started raking!

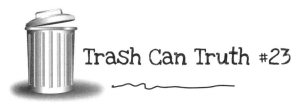

Trash Can Truth #23

Rotten food never begs to be thrown out of a refrigerator.

Rotten food is content to stay in my refrigerator until it runs me out of the kitchen. To eliminate the stench, I must look at each item to determine which ones are rotten, and which ones are worth keeping. Then, I have to manually remove the rotten ones. No gadget has been invented to do that for me.

Likewise, to assume 100% responsibility for our mental and emotional garbage, we must choose on purpose to look at every thought—tossing out the negative ones and deliberately choosing to:

- Think positive thoughts.

- Say positive words.

- Perform positive actions.

Your mind objects, "I'm in the middle of a major negative! The tornado blew our house down! Disease is destroying my body! Don't you get it, Janie? My ship is going down! I'm sinking in a sea of troubles, and you still expect me to be positive?!"

Yes! The sooner we make the shift from negative to positive, the sooner our ship can dock at a safe harbor.

Negative thoughts have to go! Negative feelings must be redirected. Negative experiences must be put behind us. We cannot nurse them, meditate on them, or talk about them repeatedly. Why? Because they cripple our resolve, destroy our hope, and defeat our spirits. In that weak state, we don't "feel like" thinking positive thoughts, speaking positive words, or performing any positive actions!

Here's our challenge: Negative feelings and the need to be positive "rub" against each other and cause real friction between what we *know to do and what we feel like doing!* How do we escape this "Catch 22?"

Solution: Take charge of your thoughts. Focus all your energy on positives. Feelings don't exist in a vacuum. Emotions don't float randomly through our bloodstream and pop into our conscious minds at will. Feelings and emotions are created by thoughts. Repeat that last sentence out loud, if you will. *Feelings and emotions are created by thoughts.* I'm telling you the truth. Love is not hanging out in your elbow. Happiness is not lodged in your knee. Sorrow is not encamped in your pancreas. **Emotions like happiness, joy, sorrow, and sadness cannot exist until a *thought* gives life to them.**

If we feel anything in our spirits, we first had a thought. If garbage is building up inside of us, and we feel anger, frustration, sadness, depression, discouragement, and other negative feelings, the best way to rid ourselves of that garbage is to change our thinking. Changing our thinking is a simple process; don't make it difficult. You're thinking one thing, and then you stop thinking that, and start thinking something else.

I've had hundreds of opportunities to practice this concept since Dickie died. One unguarded thought about missing him or needing him or what we used to do or had planned to do, and instantly, grief resurfaces and tears flow.

The Holy Bible teaches, "As a man thinketh in his heart, so is he."[1] Think positive thoughts; have positive emotions. Think negative thoughts; have negative emotions. Explanations can't get any simpler than that.

Negative thoughts have the power to create major negative garbage.

Changing our thinking is a simple process; don't make it difficult.

On one occasion, my negative thoughts almost led to a major conflict with my husband. Dickie was a neat nick. He believed that everything should have a place and be in its place when not in use. Newspapers, when not being read, should be folded and left in a certain place by the coffee table. Placemats belong on dining tables one-half inch from the edge. Occasional chairs have specific places to be as indicated by depressions in the carpet. And so it was with *every item in our house*.

This philosophy, when kept in balance, is good. Rooms remain neat and organized. Keys are easily located. However, this predisposition to neatness becomes a glaring source of contention when it gets out of balance.

Dickie had returned from a five-day trip when my thoughts about this otherwise good habit turned negative. I was in the kitchen preparing our evening meal when he came in the back door. In customary procedure, he put his suitcase down and began to hug and kiss…our dog. That was fine with me. We didn't have children, and we both loved our dog.

What followed was amazing. I did receive a quick hug and a slight peck before he started down the hallway to begin the process of putting his suitcase items back in their proper places. (No trip is over until the suitcase is unpacked.) He changed clothes and came to the kitchen, where he proceeded to touch the placemats and candlesticks, fluff the pillows on the couch, refold the newspaper, etc., as though the house were in disarray—which it was not!

Janie and Dickie with Gucci, their Italian greyhound

For the first time, the negative thought came to me. *This man is strange. He's been gone from his wife, whom he says he loves and misses when he's gone, for five days, but he's more concerned about touching items in his house than touching her.* I told Dickie my observation, and he made some feeble response, but now the thought had life. I had not only thought it, but spoken it out loud. Spoken words can become self-fulfilling prophesies.

As time passed, I began to notice more occasions when Dickie seemed to be touching things far too much. I told a friend who has a collection of medical books about my thoughts on his habit, and she found a medical condition for it—obsessive compulsive disorder. In the book, we read when the condition becomes extreme, the person could be dangerous to himself or others.

**Now the thought had life.
I had not only thought it, but spoken
it out loud. Spoken words can
become self-fulfilling prophesies.**

Now I was worried. I began thinking about how I would convince Dickie to seek counseling. Thankfully, in the middle of this mental frenzy, I was prompted to **pause and think some new thoughts**. Some of those new thoughts were: *What will happen, Janie, if you pursue this line of thinking? Where will it lead? Apart from touching things unnecessarily, does Dickie do anything that seems reasonable and good? Can you think* *on those things? Is it possible you have allowed your imagination to run wild? Could it be this will always remain the harmless habit Dickie has had since the day you first met him? Could you possibly be making too much of this?*

By changing my thoughts, I was able to win the mental battle and prevent a war.

As these new thoughts filled my mind, I realized that it was me, not Dickie, who had gotten out of balance. When I started to think of the evidence that proved Dickie's sanity, I quickly repented. Dickie was highly intelligent and well educated. He took good care of me; he bought me beautiful gifts; he was generous and kind. He went to church and prayed with me. He worked hard in his job and was highly respected as a professional. I could go on!

Once I decided to look for positive thoughts, positive thoughts started tumbling into my mind faster than I could process them. One negative thought had consumed my attention for days, but once I chose to look for positive ones, I found plenty.

What I had experienced was a mental battle—a war of thoughts—far from harmless. The thoughts were leading me to take an action, which, most likely, would have resulted in an argument. By changing my thoughts, I was able to win the mental battle and prevent a war.

How many unnecessary negatives have you created in your mind? How many unfounded fears have you generated? How many times did you feel slighted when, indeed, no harm was intended? How many experiences have you blown out of proportion just because you mediated on them too much? Are you ready to assume responsibility for those feelings?

Trash Can Truth #24

Dumpsters are located near large businesses.

If Victor Frankl could take 100% responsibility for his feelings, we have no excuses, though Victor needed more than a trash can. He needed a dumpster. You see, Frankl was a doctor imprisoned in a Nazi concentration camp during World War II. His captors beat him and tortured him, stripped him of his clothing, starved him, and left him for long periods in solitary confinement, sleeping in his own body's wastes.

Victor Frankl had lost control of everything he held dear. The Nazis had taken all of his possessions, and could take his very life at a moment's notice. He wanted to die. Then he realized he did possess some things the Nazis could not take: his *attitude* and his *thoughts*.

Though he had lost control of what happened to him physically, the meanest Nazi could not get inside his head. Frankl realized he had perfect control of his thoughts. By having control of his thoughts, he could also control his feelings. He was the sole owner and master of his inner life! Try as they may, the Nazis could not make him hate them.

In life, attitude is not everything; but attitude does determine how much we enjoy everything.

With his new-found power, Frankl began to forgive and love his captors. He returned kindness and respect for their ugliness. Miraculously, Victor Frankl survived the concentration camp experience, and lived to write the book *Man's Search for Meaning*. In it he described this great human power—the power to choose what we think and how we feel.[2]

In life, attitude is not everything; but attitude does determine how much we enjoy everything. We have to become like Mike, the man who fell out of a window on the top floor of a twenty-story building. As he passed the fourteenth floor, a friend yelled, "Hey, Mike. How's it going?" Mike replied, "So far so good." Though Mike's future seemed doomed, no one really knows the future. **We have learned, however, that though a positive attitude may not change our destiny, it will help us enjoy the journey.**

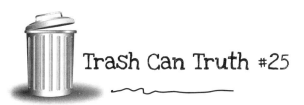

Trash Can Truth #25

Even garbage collectors take breaks.

Though armed with a positive attitude, garbage collecting can still be exhausting. We need to refresh ourselves with periodic breaks.

Built into the contracts for most city waste management specialists is a clause that specifies a certain number of breaks during the work day for each employee. We innately understand, whether laws dictate it or not, that people can only focus intently on a task for so long, and then they need a break.

Assuming responsibility for our feelings means that we sometimes have to relax and take a break. We have to know our limits and protect ourselves. Most people don't mean us any harm, but they don't always know what's going on inside of us. What seems to others like an insignificant comment could cut us to the bone. Our emotions could be hemorrhaging on the inside and nobody would know it.

Every college football team has its favorite stories of years gone by, and the Ole Miss Rebels from the University of Mississippi are no different. In 1948 the Rebels played the LSU Tigers and won 49 to 19. Every offensive back on the Rebel team scored that day except halfback Billy Mustin.

Quarterback Farley "Fish" Salmon urged Mustin to get in on the action by handing him the ball every time the Rebels were in scoring range. Mustin said later, "It was wearing me out. I got knocked out three times."

When Billy took a lick to his head a third time, he went out on the LSU side and sat on the Tigers' bench. One of the coaches said to him, "Son, we don't mind you being here, but did you know you're on the Tiger bench?" Billy said, "Coach, I know it. But if I go out to the Rebel bench, they'll put me back in the game."[3]

Billy knew no one understood how he felt but him. Legendary Coach Johnny Vaught cared greatly about his players, but he didn't feel Billy's pain and confusion at the time. Billy needed a break, and he took one.

Let Billy's story be yours. **When you know you**

need a break, take one. Let's not keep pushing until we lose our sense of humor, get grumpy, and start complaining. Let's not serve and care for others, suffering in silence, until we're sick in our spirits and mad at everyone around us. Take a break!

If we're not watchful, we won't even notice we're sinking into negativity.

Perhaps the most stressful job in the entire world is president of the United States, but even presidents take breaks. We see them on national television jogging, riding horses, sailing boats, golfing, playing trumpets, petting dogs, and other stress-relieving activities. That's good!

Emotional responsibility means paying attention to how we feel, being selective about what we think, and choosing not to be a part of things that can hurt us. If we're not watchful, we won't even notice we're sinking into negativity. Disappointments, hurts, complaints, exhaustion, and the like, slip in slowly—a little here, a little there—and before we know it…kerplunk! We're in an emotional pit.

When you feel the pressure building, take a break!

Play a game, call a friend, read a good book, go for a walk, take a vacation. Now that's the idea I like the best—take a vacation. This book has been partially written while I've been on vacation.

On one such writing excursion, I arrived in Seaside, Florida, so physically and emotionally spent, I cried three times the first day there for no reason at all. I sang a familiar hymn and cried; I saw a stray dog and cried; I read one paragraph in a book and had to put it down because tears blurred my vision.

When you feel the pressure building, take a break!

Now get this, friends. I am not a cry baby. Prior to Dickie's death, I rarely ever cried. In the first place, I wear entirely too much makeup to cry. Wet mascara makes a huge mess. In the second place, crying gives me a sinus headache. If I have a problem, the last thing I want to do is cry about it, 'cause then I'll have two issues—the problem and a headache!

On this occasion, I realized before I typed a single word during this writing retreat, I needed to take a break! I went to a worship service, watched a great movie,

October Skies, worked out at the fitness center, soaked in a Jacuzzi, ate pizza and salad in a down-home, casual atmosphere, went to bed early, and slept late the next day. By the time my laptop was turned on, so was I. Be smart. Even garbage collectors take breaks.

Trash Can Truth #26

The garbage truck comes only one time to each house on collection day.

Grocery stores, gasoline stations, and hospitals are open 24/7. We can make several trips to them each day, and no one complains. Garbage collection is different. My garbage is collected on Tuesday and again on Friday. The collection trucks will come to my house only one time on each of those days. If I miss the pick-up time, I must hang on to that garbage until the next collection day.

Life truly is a great deal like garbage collecting. When opportunity knocks on our heart's door and announces, "I'm collecting garbage today," we must seize that opportunity right then. **Don't wait. Don't hold on to the negativity for one more tour through self-pity.**

Once we decide to go forward with a negative thought, changing in midstream is difficult. Like missing our exit on the interstate, we sometimes must drive several miles before we have a chance to turn around.

When opportunity knocks on our heart's door and announces, "I'm collecting garbage today," we must seize that opportunity right then.

As an example, I'm thinking of the husband and wife who start with complaining and faultfinding, and move to accusing and threatening, and, before you know it, divorce proceedings are underway. Neither party really wants a divorce, but stopping the process is difficult. Many ugly things have been said and done at this point. The same is true of the employee and employer who complain and point fingers and demand and threaten, and before you know it, another worker is looking for a job, and a boss is trying to find someone to fill a good employee's shoes. Neither one really wanted this, but one thing led to another….

If only the people in these examples would have bailed out of the negative thinking the first time opportunity knocked, and said, "I'm collecting garbage today." But no, our proud warriors held on to their garbage and proceeded to generate even more.

Thankfully, human beings are not interstate highways. As soon as we realize we've missed our exit, we can turn around! We can change our thinking!

I remember a time Dickie and I went on a cruise that sailed out of New Orleans. My mother had just died after a lengthy illness, and Dickie thought it would be good for me to get away and unwind. The cruise included a couple of days on the water, three days touring islands, and a couple of days coming back to port.

This incident occurred on the first day of our return trip. After three days of snorkeling, shopping, and sightseeing, I decided to relax in the cabin. The in-room television programming featured the movie, *Hope Floats*. I hadn't seen it, but several friends who had seen the movie loved it.

As I settled in, the beginning scene disturbed me quite a bit. The husband was revealing to his wife an ugly infidelity on television in front of an audience. That resulted in the wife packing the couple's only daughter into a car and heading back to Mama. I thought to myself, *why did he do that? His wife hadn't run up his credit cards or let herself become physically unattractive. He's a jerk.* But I continued to watch the movie.

When the wife returned to her childhood home, her relationship with her mother was strained. They argued and nagged each other. I felt a tinge of sadness begin. Remember, I had just lost my mother, and I thought, *if she knew how precious her mother really was to her, she wouldn't be talking to her that way.* But I continued to watch the movie.

Thankfully, human beings are not interstate highways. As soon as we realize we've missed our exit, we can turn around! We can change our thinking!

The next scene that blew me away occurred when the husband visited and asked the wife for a divorce. I saw that coming. What I didn't see coming was that memorable scene when the little daughter follows her daddy to his car. As the father drives away, the little girl screams, "Daddy, please don't leave me!" Every muscle in my body tightened. My thoughts began to race around the world and grieve for all the children who have had their very foundations ripped out from under them by divorce. The drama continued to unfold.

The final blow came to my already depressed psyche when the older mother—the only person in the entire movie who had any sense—died. What had my mother just done—died?! My breathing became shallow, my body recoiled, and I was within seconds of bursting into tears—a crying, blubbering fit.

Remember now, tears come to me at great personal sacrifice. My eyes swell, my sinuses clog, my nose runs, and my head throbs for hours. I resort to tears only when I'm at the end of my rope, and I have no other release for the emotion but to let it flow out through my tear ducts.

> **In the midst of the worst possible garbage, if we can search for or generate one positive thought, we can bag that trash and get it out of our lives!**

As I sat in that beautiful cabin, searching for a way to avoid this onslaught of sobbing, the Holy Spirit sent me one interrupting thought. Not a barrage of thoughts, just one thought…one chance to bail out of this sinking emotional ship…one exit on the interstate of life (smile). But thankfully, that's all it takes, just one positive thought. Oh, the power of one! In the midst of the worse possible garbage, if we can search for, or generate, one positive thought, we can bag that trash and get it out of our lives!

The one thought that came floating into the midst of my sea of sadness was a question: *Janie, is this really the direction you want to go in today?* That was it. The garbage truck was at my mental house. Here was my one and only chance to bail out of a horrendous headache!

I thought about the question for a few seconds and then I shouted, "No! I paid a thousand dollars to come on this cruise, and I didn't come here to cry about all the sadness in the world, with all of its disadvantaged children and death. I came here to relax and have fun!"

I got up that very second and turned off the TV. I put on nine layers of makeup, the brightest outfit I brought, and left the cabin. I went up on deck and found myself a Jamaican man playing steel drums. I asked him how they worked, and he gave me a free lesson. Others on the ship gathered around. We laughed, pounded out rhythms, and danced to the Macarena. I felt empowered and energized, and I created for myself and others a good time. Lying in bed that night, I thanked God for the gift of one positive thought! I also thanked Him for the good sense to seize it!

Do you remember the line I asked you to repeat earlier in this chapter? *Feelings and emotions are created by thoughts.* It's true! No one can think your thoughts but you. Your thoughts create your feelings. That makes you and me 100% responsible for our emotions. Good news! Tomorrow the garbage trucks run. Be your best friend. Bag your negative thoughts today, and haul them to the street!

CHAPTER NINE

Cleaning Agent #6:
Practice the Magic of "Acting As If..."

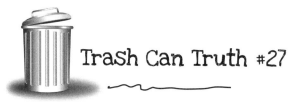

Trash Can Truth #27

Though not illusion or sleight of hand,
a positive attitude toward much of our
garbage can make it disappear.

I knew it was time for a major job change the day my high school theatre students won first place at the State Drama Festival. On that day, the dread of raising money to get the students to the next level—the Southeastern Theater Conference—was greater than the thrill of victory. In spite of the dread, the students were excited; I had a job to do, so I started acting like I was excited, too. I kept acting until the money was raised, the trip was made, and we had a glorious experience to remember. Dread had totally disappeared!

If you want to pull yourself out of the doldrums

when unhappy negatives attack, start talking and acting as though you are already happy, and the feeling of happiness will surely follow. By acting in a positive, optimistic way, we can shrink any garbage down to size.

How do we "act" happy? Come on, you know. We smile, talk cheerfully and optimistically, laugh, hum, walk with a fast step, stand up straight, and hold our chins high. We look upward.

By acting in a positive, optimistic way, we can shrink any garbage down to size.

As far-fetched as it sounds, this cleaning agent is incredibly effective at ridding us of mental and emotional garbage. We can indeed act happy, and, in a short time, produce happiness, or any other emotion we desire, based on how we act. Most actions require thought which produces feelings!

If you don't like gathering your garbage and taking it to the curb, act like you do. Put a smile on your face, and whistle a happy tune as you walk to the street. Likewise, in life, if you don't like some aspect of your job but must do it anyway, smile and act like you enjoy it. If you're fearful about giving a presentation but must deliver it anyway, smile and act like you're confident. **Literally, anything you must do, whether you want to do it or not, will benefit from this powerful cleaning agent—the magic of acting as if!**

Tackle any "must do" garbage with a happy face, and a better outcome can be expected. Three German scientists proved this in a fascinating study about smiles. They wanted to discover if the expression on your face had any influence on the attitude in your heart—our perceived enjoyment of life.

They divided their participants into two groups. Each group was shown the same set of fourteen cartoons. The participants were asked to rate how funny they thought the cartoons were. One group, while look-ing at the cartoons, was asked to hold a pen between their teeth, not allowing their lips to touch it. The pen grasped in their teeth created a forced smile on each face. No emotion was involved in the experiment, just the forced smile caused by a pen.

The other group, while also attempting to rate the humor value of the cartoons, was instructed to hold the pen in their mouths using only their lips, not allow-ing their teeth to touch it. The pen, held by their lips, resulted in a forced frown. Like the first group, no internal emotion was involved in the experiment. The frown was forced onto the face by the pen. With pens in mouths, both groups rated how funny they thought the cartoons were.

A smile on your face can help produce a positive attitude—a favorable outlook toward life.

Overall, the group that was smiling while they looked at the cartoons gave the cartoons funnier ratings than the frowning group.[1] Remember, the cartoons were the same for both groups; only the facial expressions changed. Conclusion: A smile on your face can help produce a positive attitude—a favorable outlook toward life. **Whether you're happy or not, put a smile on your face. Make physiology work for you!**

My own experience reinforces this truth. In the South, when we are around people we like, but don't see often, we encourage them to visit us by saying, "If you're ever in my neighborhood, why don't you stop by?" Though generally a sincere invitation, we rarely expect anyone to do it.

One Saturday morning I awoke exhausted from several continuous weeks of a demanding schedule. I had looked forward to this day, expecting to do nothing but sleep and eat and watch television. I had even banished my husband from the couch—his typical Saturday morning perch for watching cooking and art shows. The couch was to be mine.

The thought never occurred to me that if I acted energized, I could feel energized and enjoy the day.

Still in my bathrobe, with no make-up on, I looked out my living room window and saw a strange car in the driveway. A closer look revealed a dear lady in my community who had "stopped by to visit." My heart sank. I almost ran to the bedroom and shut the door, pretending no one was home; but I had invited her, and she was a sweet lady, so I went to the door, put on a cheerful face, and greeted my friend.

For the next twenty to thirty minutes, we sipped hot lemon zinger tea, and laughed and chatted. When she was ready to leave, I walked her to the door, thanked her for coming, and headed back to my couch. Strangely,

I felt too good to "veg-out" on the couch. My energy renewed, I got dressed, got active, and had a most productive day.

Think of it! I had actually planned in advance to have a bum day. The thought never occurred to me that if I acted energized, I could feel energized and enjoy the day. Thankfully, the "act" became my reality.

Trash Can Truth #28

Around 1350, Britain introduced their first official garbage men—called "rakers." Their job was simply to rake trash into a cart on a weekly basis.[2]

Shakespeare's Juliet, in the play bearing her name, declares "a rose by any other name would smell as sweet." That philosophy applies well to roses, but not to everything. As a matter of fact, many things in life, when you change the name, you elevate the subject, change the potential, enlarge its future, and redirect its path. It can smell sweeter. Call a greasy spoon of a restaurant an atmospheric café with local charm, and you've changed, elevated, enlarged, and redirected its future. Call a faded, chipped mixing bowl a cherished antique that produces loving memories of grandma's biscuits, and it, too, has increased in sweeter importance.

"Acting as if" everything is going to be fine by taking positive actions and speaking positive words in the middle of negatives is not just a poetic or New Age tactic. This principle is based on scriptures straight from the Bible. In Genesis, God changed Abram's name to Abraham, which means "father of many nations." God did this long before Abraham even fathered one child, let alone a nation. But every time the people called him Abraham, they were speaking into his spirit the hope of God's promise—father to many nations.[3]

For many things in life, when you change the name, you elevate the subject, change the potential, enlarge its future, and redirect its path.

Another scripture teaches us, "Let the weak say I am strong."[4] Why? Words have creative power. **We are created in God's image, empowered by His Spirit. Since God spoke this world into existence, we, like Him, can speak our worlds into existence.** God cares about our words. King David sang in one of his psalms, "May the words of my mouth and the meditations of my heart be acceptable in Thy sight, O Lord, my Strength and my Redeemer."[5] I seriously doubt God appreciates words of ugliness, defeat, and despair.

After Moses' death, when Joshua started to lead the children of Israel across the Jordan River into the Promised Land, the Jordan River was overflowing its banks. I'm sure some in the crowd thought Joshua was crazy. He told the people to pack their gear and get ready to move. He instructed the priests to lead the procession across the river.

The first row of priests led off with their marching foot and stepped into the water. The entire entourage fully "acted as if" they were going to walk across the Jordan River. You know what? They did! As soon as the priests' feet hit the water, the waters of the Jordan parted and the Israelites walked across on dry land.[6] Yes, those people were part of a miracle. Perhaps that's why I think this tool is so powerful. To some degree, "acting as if" all is well (before all is actually well) allows us to be a part of little miracles.

One such little miracle occurred for me in the Dallas-Fort Worth airport. My plane was cancelled due to stormy weather. Though I had the option of going to a hotel (with only a little time for actual sleep), I opted to remain at the airport, now filled with hundreds of disgruntled passengers.

"Acting as if" this was a great adventure, I embarked on the night with enthusiasm. Thanks to the goodness of God, I found an empty lounge chair in a passenger waiting room, and claimed it for the night. At midnight, after visiting with the dozen or so people around me, I set an alarm clock, placed a scarf over my eyes, and slept for five uninterrupted hours. I awoke semi-refreshed, having enjoyed the whole experience. I'm confident "acting as if" I was going to have a good experience helped produce the result!

To some degree, "acting as if" all is well (before all is actually well) allows us to be a part of little miracles.

Religion is certainly not the only place we find the instruction to "call those things that be not as though they were."[7] The world of the theatre, since its inception, has operated under this principle, and actually coined the phrase, "the magic of acting as if." Centuries of theatre enthusiasts have sat in arenas of various shapes, watched as the story begins, and been drawn into the action on the stage or screen, totally suspending their sense of reality. The audience was pretending as if what they saw was real. Today the pretense thrives.

Millions of people annually listen and watch intently as actors perform, allowing them to become, in our minds, the real people their characters portray. We know their characters are not the "real people," and their "living rooms" are not in "real houses," but we willingly agree to suspend our disbelief.

We laugh and cry with them. We gasp in horror and squeal with delight as both tragedy and comedy enter their lives.

Night after night—sometimes running on Broadway for years—the live theatre casts its magic spell on audiences, transforming them from mere spectators into emotional players gazing through the imaginary fourth wall of the stage—watching the actors practice the magic of "acting as if."

In a theatrical sense, what does it mean…"acting as if?" It's simple. Though the butler rehearsed the scene a hundred times, during opening night he "acts as if" he's shocked when he opens the front door on stage and discovers Sir Winston O'Neill, his long, lost master, presumed dead, standing on the porch.

In another performance, we watch through veiled

shadows as Elvira stumbles and tumbles, then mumbles about the fall, only to gasp with her as she finds the light and sees the gruesome corpse lying on the floor. Though this scene was carefully staged and rehearsed to avoid injury, Elvira "acts as if" she's as surprised as we are by the sight.

I had to do the best I could with what I had! That's what "acting as if" is really all about.

The "magic of acting as if" enabled the butler and Elvira to usher us into their imaginary worlds. What a magnificent tool for neutralizing negatives. "Acting as if" helps define not only the emotions of the actors, but those watching the actor, as well.

If we really want to rid ourselves of mental and emotional garbage, we need to start pretending we can easily handle the garbage and, if that is too much of a stretch for our imaginations, we should at least pretend in such a way as to shrink the negatives down to size.

Several years ago I invited one of the ministers at my church and his wife for dinner. Though not known for my baking, I found a chocolate pie recipe that looked fabulous in the magazine. I doubled the ingredients so I'd be sure to have leftovers and cooked the pie filling for what seemed like an hour, but it never thickened! Finally, I poured the filling into the pie crust, hoping it would become firm as it cooled.

To my dismay, the filling was still not firm when it came time to serve the pie. Like any good cook, I crumbled the crust and filling together, put it in bowls, and "acted as if" pudding was what I had intended to serve all along! As expected, all four bowls were quickly emptied by my complimentary guests.

A runny pie filling is not what I'd call mental or emotional garbage, but the principle is the same. What I had was not what I wanted, but there was nothing I could do at the time to change it. I had to do the best I could with what I had! That's what "acting as if" is really all about.

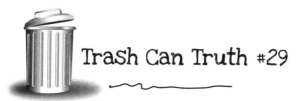

Trash Can Truth #29

Garbage piled on the side of the road becomes debris in the middle of the road.

Sometimes the odd shapes of our garbage won't fit neatly into cans, so what is a body to do? Pile the garbage in a heap beside the road so everyone can see it? No! My experience has been that garbage left unattached on the side of the road can become debris in the middle of the road.

That scenario parallels our day-to-day grind. Many chores in life are unpleasant, and responsibilities often occur at inconvenient times. They don't fit neatly into our job descriptions and calendars, a.k.a. bags and cans. Instead of acting as if we're pleased to do them, we spend our time balking and complaining, never making peace with the intruding task. We make sure everyone in earshot knows of our burden to bear. We figuratively pile our resentment on the side of the road for all to see, and our attitude pollutes the nearby areas.

I'm as guilty as the next person. I hate hauling water hoses all over a yard. That chore is major garbage to me. Though Dickie did the majority of this task, I hated any portion of it that fell my lot. Most memorably, the irrigation system in our yard in Gulfport lasted only two years before the pipes were clogged and the plastic parts were broken. The sandy soil didn't hold water long, so watering the plants was an every-other-day job at the very least, and, because of the summer heat, some flowers needed water daily. That meant water hoses had to be repositioned all over the yard.

I never managed to set the sprinklers without getting wet. Soggy shoes were common, and what the sprinklers didn't ruin of my makeup, the sweat running down my face did. Probably the worst part of all was that the flowers were not my idea. My idea of a beautiful lawn is what one gentleman did when he covered his lawn in concrete, painted it green, and bolted his lawn mower to the concrete with a sign that read: "Rust in peace."

Grumbling about the chore, however, never made it go away, but you can be sure I grumbled. I piled my attitudinal garbage on the side of the road so all could see. I made sure I told the neighbors across the street and the ones next door how I felt about this chore. Total strangers would pass by on the sidewalk, and I'd greet them with an invitation to come help me. I'd let them do it all if they'd like.

We figuratively pile our resentment on the side of the road for all to see, and our attitude pollutes the nearby areas.

The only thing that ever helped me manage the frustration was those rare times I put a smile on my face, and acted as if I enjoyed it. Those times occurred when special visitors were present. I couldn't let them see "Miss Optimism" fussing, now could I? The wet shoes and smudged makeup never seemed to be problems those days.

Why didn't I connect the dots? If I could pretend I enjoyed moving water hoses when I had spectators, I could have pretended and acted like I enjoyed it every day. I wish I had known then what I know now. The pretense would have eventually produced contentment with the task, instead of disdain. I haven't needed to haul a water hose for a long time now. Should the opportunity—yes, opportunity—ever present itself, I look forward to fully enjoying the experience. I'm determined to pretend I like it, and I will!

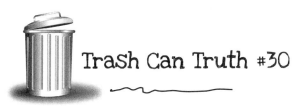

Trash Can Truth #30

Every year Americans use approximately one billion plastic shopping bags, creating 300,000 tons of landfill waste.[8]

Like small, plastic shopping bags, the little bits of negativity exhibited by people throughout a day can create a heavy atmosphere for everyone. Many of those seemingly innocent negative attitudes can be eliminated, or at least neutralized, by applying this simple cleaning agent.

Since my watering days, I've had plenty of other occasions to test this "acting as if" principle. **In testing it, I discovered that pretending all is well often benefits not only us, but the people around us. When we take a negative experience or task and put a positive twist on it, our positive attitude brightens**

the atmosphere for everyone involved, just as the environment is healthier with one less plastic bag in the ground, and the air is cleaner with one less pollutant.

To illustrate, I remember an occasion when pretending I was happy reaped an ample supply of happiness for me, and started a chain reaction of happiness for others.

A student who was faithful to my high school theatre program landed a leading role in a college production of a play billed as a comedy. He was eager for me to see him perform, and I really wanted to go, but…. My excuses were numerous: I had afternoon rehearsals for a play I was directing; I had papers to grade; and, like most teachers, I was tired! Earlier though, I had given the student my word I would attend. He had arranged complimentary tickets for Dickie and me, so staying home was not an option.

When the play began, the actors were doing a great job, but for some reason the audience was shy about laughing and applauding. Maybe they were all tired like me. Nonetheless, I was determined to help my student as much as I could, so I began to act like I was really into the show. I laughed at every opportunity and applauded at every scene change. In just a few short scenes, the rest of the audience warmed up, and we were all laughing heartily by the end of the show!

Dickie and I fully enjoyed the evening. When I arrived at the theater, I could barely drag myself from the parking lot to the auditorium. When the play was over, I practically skipped back to the car. Dickie and I hardly spoke a word to each other during the drive to the theater, but returning home, we laughed and chatted all the way.

What made the difference? Pretending made the difference—acting as if we were having a good time. Those good feelings came not just for us, but for the ones around us.

What made the difference? Pretending made the difference—acting as if we were having a good time. When we got our actions right, the good feelings came. Those good feelings came not just for us, but for the ones around us. That audience was made up of good people who just needed someone to ignite the spark of enjoyment. By consistently "acting as if" I was into the play, that spark was fanned into a flame that allowed other people to share the fire.

Trash Can Truth #31

Garbage is more appealing to the senses when corralled in decorative containers.

My kitchen is usually a disaster after I've hosted a party. Empty cans, two-liter bottles, disposable platters, paper towels, and food scraps are but some of the garbage scattered on countertops. Within minutes, though, all that clutter can be hidden in a plastic bag, and tucked away in an artfully decorated kitchen garbage can, protecting guests from the unsightly mess. The can doesn't eliminate the garbage, but it does cover it up and make the atmosphere better for everyone until the garbage is carried to the curb.

Likewise, saying what we want to be true, instead of what we feel to be true, is somewhat like putting garbage in attractive cans. A nice-looking can doesn't eliminate the garbage, but it does make the garbage more pleasant to be around.

As I travel across America, I hear one repetitive complaint about southerners. "You people in the South aren't honest," they say. "You smile at someone and tell them you don't mind being interrupted, when in reality the interruption was a major annoyance. You tell them you're happy to help them do whatever, when you really think they could do it by themselves if they just would. What's up with you southerners?"

A nice-looking can doesn't eliminate the garbage, but it does make the garbage more pleasant to be around.

I'm not convinced southerners are the only ones in the country who do this, but we are guilty. That willingness to help is all about hospitality, for which we are known. Chances are, if you ask most decent citizens to do something, they're going to do it if they can. Since we're going to do it anyway, doesn't it make good sense to say, "We'll be happy to do it," rather than griping and complaining about the intrusion?

Saying "we'll be happy" figuratively places a pretty bag over the task at hand, covering up even the slightest reluctant spirit that feels the suffering of an imposition. The person receiving the good deed or kind word is grateful. Tension is almost always reduced and a pleasant atmosphere preserved when help is offered with a positive attitude. The huge advantage, though, is reserved for the person doing the job. We said we'd be happy, and our subconscious mind heard us.

I once heard it explained that our subconscious is like an engineer in the boiler room of a big ship. When the captain calls down through the intercom system and says, "All ahead full," the engineer can't see anything. He only hears his orders from the captain and performs them. Likewise, my subconscious only hears what I tell it and obediently starts moving in that direction. **If my subconscious hears "I'm happy," it will start working to make my statement a reality.**

Trash Can Truth #32

Using cheap garbage bags creates twice the work—initially gathering the garbage, then picking it up again after the bag breaks.

I hear your protests. You say, "Janie, there's garbage, and then there's real garbage. Will this principle of *speaking the truth you want and "acting as if" everything is okay* work on the tough things in life? Are there garbage bags big enough to make crippling accidents and heartbreaking relationships more pleasant to be around? Is it possible to corral the tension in the atmosphere when you've lost your job, or when the diagnosis is bad, simply by "acting as if" everything is going to be fine?" Yes! But really tough garbage requires really strong bags.

A strong bag is a true commitment to optimism—a true commitment, not just a passing positive thought, followed by frantic worry and doubt. **The "act" must be sustained! Figuratively speaking, the *performance* must be prepared for a long run on Broadway.**

In his book, *Good to Great,* Jim Collins records an interview with Admiral Jim Stockdale. Admiral Stockdale was the highest ranking officer in the Hanoi prisoner-of-war camp during the Vietnam War. The interview tells of the personal abuses done to the Admiral and of the many heroic feats the Admiral accomplished while in captivity.

Toward the end of the session, Jim Collins, now sobered by all he has heard, asked the Admiral what type of men didn't survive the prison. The Admiral replied with little hesitation, "The optimists." He explained the optimists were the ones who expected to be liberated quickly, but the long months of imprisonment dashed their hopes. Stockdale said these would-be optimists died of broken hearts. The interview ended with the admonition that to be a true optimist, **we must never lose faith in the truth that we will succeed in the end.**[9]

Yes, it is possible to bag the garbage created by bitter, hateful words spoken to you by a friend in a fit of anger. We can bag that garbage by saying, "I will walk in forgiveness." These words and deeds must be more than a passing sentiment. They must be supported by a true commitment to healing and peace. They must be repeated daily, accompanied by kindness and smiles, until the forgiveness is fully complete in our hearts.

> **These words and deeds must be more than a passing sentiment. They must be supported by a true commitment to healing and peace.**

Yes, it is possible to bag the garbage left by the pink slip ending your career when the business outsources your position. A confidence in your skills, a strong faith in the God who supplies all your needs,[10] and a determination to persist until you land a better job can all be sustained with words like, "All things will work together for my good,"[11] or "I was looking for a job when I found this one. I'll find another one." We must keep the "act" of positive speaking going until another job is found.

Quite frankly, when my cherished Dickie died suddenly of a heart attack on March 22, 2010, my grief and despair were too great for even the strongest plastic containers. Those emotions required steel vaults to contain them. I capped that garbage can with the same advice I'm offering you—I started acting and talking as though I was going to be all right.

The stage is set. The director is calling for you. "Places, everyone!" The curtain is opening. It's show time!

I would get up every morning and inhale and exhale and say to myself, "Janie, you can do this." Though healing did take time, I eventually started to look forward, not backward. Instead of saying, "I'm all alone," I started saying, "I'm now free to go wherever God leads." Instead of crying on the back pew of church, I started singing praise songs in the choir loft. Instead of sitting home alone, I started traveling to visit friends and inviting neighbors over for dinner. By doing so, I eventually emptied my heart and mind of the mental and emotional garbage that comes with the loss of anything precious. I started "acting as if" I was fine, and today I am.

It's now your turn. The stage is set. The director

is calling for you. "Places, everyone!" The curtain is opening. It's show time! Start your *miracle* right this minute by "acting as if…"

CHAPTER TEN

All Six Cleaning Agents in One Small Chapter

Now you have them...all six of the handy cleaning agents I use to neutralize the negatives in my life. Let me list these tools for you once again.

#1: Be willing to change your perspectives and look at negative situations from positive angles.

#2: Adopt the Golden Rule. Start doing for other people what you would like to have them do for you. The good that you send out will surely come back to you in most delightful ways.

#3: Maintain good self-esteem and good self-worth. Never let what happens to you diminish who you are. Highlight all you are capable of doing. Remember you are loved by a holy God who created you. He values you and has good plans for your life.

#4: Laugh, and laugh often. Laughter is truly good medicine for the body and soul of mankind.

#5: Assume responsibility for your feelings. If you're angry, accept the fact that you choose to be angry. You do have options. If you're depressed, you choose to be depressed by thinking on negatives instead of celebrating positives. If you're joyful, you choose to be joyful.

#6: "Act as if" you're happy, and keep acting until the charade becomes reality. Feelings do follow actions. Happiness will emerge.

Using these six tools, I've been able to go from a teacher of speech to a professional speaker, from barren to fulfilled, from widow to wonder woman, wondering what new and exciting challenges and adventures await me, what meaningful service I can render today.

Though the garbage truck comes to my house on Tuesdays and Fridays, any day is a good day to collect trash, put it in a bag, and get it out of our lives. Negative feelings and emotions start to contaminate us the minute they enter our minds and hearts. Don't wait to start using this handy six-pack. Go ahead. Today is garbage day. Start collecting! Let's bag it! We've got a lot of living yet to do!

Endnotes

Chapter 2: You Call That Garbage?!@#?
1. Deuteronomy 30:19
2. Philippians 3:13-14
3. Psalm 51:10

Chapter 3: A Decision Is Only As Good As the Action That Supports It
1. ConsumerReports.org, "Kitchen Trash Bag Testing," May 10, 2012
2. Ziglar, Zig. *See You At the Top*. Gretna, Louisiana: Pelican Publishing Co., 1979.
3. Matthew 7:7-8

Chapter 4: Cleaning Agent #1, Change Your Perspective
1. http://www.chacha.com
2. http://www.gallap.com/poll/147887/Americans-continue-believe-god.aspx
3. Psalm 136:1
4. Matthew 28:20
5. Jeremiah 29:13
6. Hebrews 11:1
7. John 6:29
8. Hebrews 11:6
9. Environmental Protection Agency Report, "Municipal Solid Waste Generation, Recycling, and Disposal in the United States: Facts and Figures for 2010."

10. Swindoll, Charles R., American writer and clergyman. Born 1934.

11. James 3:2-4

12. 1 Kings 18:42-45

13. http://www.cancerresearchuk.org/cancer-info/cancerstats/ survival/england-
Hermann Brenner, "Long-term survival rates of cancer patients achieved by the end of the 20th century: a period analysis," the Lancet, 360 (October 12, 2002), 1131-1135

14. Genesis 1:3

15. Genesis 1:26-27

16. Waitley, Denis. *Seeds of Greatness*. Pocket Books, a div. of Simon & Schuster, Inc., New York, 1983.

17. Psalm 100:5

Chapter 5: Cleaning Agent #2, Practice the Golden Rule

1. http://www.bestbuy.com/site/KitchenAid

2. Luke 6:31

3. Udana-Varga 5:18

4. 40 Hadith of an—Nawawi 13

5. Mahabharata 5, 1517

6. Sherman, Richard M.; Sherman, Robert B. "A Spoonful of Sugar" from Walt Disney's *Mary Poppins*. Milwaukee, Wisconsin, Wonderland Music Co., Hal Leonard Distributors, 2002.

7. Galatians 6:7

8. Isaiah 43:25

9. Covanta Energy, Morristown, NJ, Email: info@covantaenergy.com

10. Rodgers, Richard; Hammerstein II, Oscar, "Do-Re-Me" from *The Sound of Music*, Williamson Music Co., New York, NY, 1959.

11. Hebrews 11:6

12. Romans 8:28

Chapter 6: Cleaning Agent #3, Maintain Good Self-Esteem

1. http://www.environmentalistseveryday.org/publications-solid-waste-industry

2. http://www.environmentalistseveryday.org/docs/research-bulletin/Research-Bulletin-Modern-Landfill.pdf

3. John 3:16

4. Deuteronomy 6:5

5. Matthew 28:19-20

6. Luke 12:7

7. Psalm 56:8

8. Jeremiah 29:11

9. Matthew 28:20

10. John 14:2

11. Maslow, Abraham. *Motivation and Personality*, 1st Ed. NY: Harper, 1954. 3rd Ed. NY: Addison-Wesley, 1987.

12. Ehrmann, Max, Poet. Desiderata,1927.

13. http://www.behealthyandrelax.com/2007/11/how-long-does-it-take-to-decompose

Chapter 7: Cleaning Agent #4, Laugh

1. Proverbs 17:22

2. Cousins, Norman. *The Anatomy of an Illness As Perceived by the Patient*. New York; Norton, 1979.

3. Ephesians 6:13

4. Metcalf, C.W.; Felible, Roma. *Lighten Up*. Massachusetts: Addison-Wesley Publishing, 1992, page 9.

5. Paper Industry Association Council, http://www.paperrecycles.org

6. Psalm 51:12

Chapter 8: Cleaning Agent #5, Assume Responsibility for Your Feelings

1. Proverbs 23:7
2. Frankl, Victor. *Man's Search for Meaning*. Revised and Updated. Beacon Press. 1959, 1962, 1984.
3. Sorrels, William W.; Cavagnaro, Charles. *Ole Miss Rebels: Mississippi Football*. The Strode Publishers, Inc., Huntsville, Alabama; 1976, pps. 159-160.

Chapter 9: Cleaning Agent #6, Practice the Magic of "Acting As If…"

1. Wikipedia, the free encyclopedia. *Facial Feedback Hypothesis*. Strack, Fritz; Martin, Leonard; Stepper, Sabine. Universitat Mannheim, Federal Republic of Germany, 1988.
2. http://www.environmentalistseveryday.org/publications-solid-waste-industry
3. Genesis 17:5
4. Joel 3:10
5. Psalm 19:14
6. Joshua 3:7-17
7. Romans 4:17
8. http://www.byui.edu/university-operations/facilities-management/recycling
9. Collins, Jim. *Good to Great*. Harper Business, 2001, pps. 83-85.
10. Philippians 4:19
11. Romans 8:28

About the Author

Janie Walters is an award-winning communications specialist. She is a master teacher with more than 25 years experience teaching interpersonal communications, public speaking, debate, and theatre at the high school and college levels. She holds B.S. and M.S. degrees in Speech Education and Communication from the University of Southern Mississippi in Hattiesburg. Champion Communications, her speaking and training service, is based in Madison, Mississippi.

Walters has spoken more than a thousand times in 42 states at national, state, and local conferences across the country spreading her messages of joy, wisdom, and communication excellence to government agencies, military bases, hospitals, churches, schools, and various associations of all sizes, moving easily from large conference stages to small meeting rooms.

Her clients include such prestigious names as the National Security Agency, American Heart Association, Federal Bureau of Investigation, Washington Naval Yard, National Kidney Foundation, Edwards Air Force Base, and the National Girl Scouts. Janie guarantees each of her audiences a potentially life-changing event filled with wholesome fun.

Janie Walters is a member of Highland Colony Baptist Church in Ridgeland, Mississippi, and speaks nationally for church events and Christian conferences. She is also the author of *Blow A Bubble Not A Gasket: 101 Ways to Reduce Stress and Add Fun to Your Life*, and *Develop the Habit of Joy*.

Champion Communications

The following keynotes and/or workshops, conducted by Janie Walters, are designed to equip people with the communication skills needed to seize the best life has to offer and to encourage people to offer their best back to life.

The Garbage Truck Comes on Tuesdays And Fridays!
Throw Mental and Emotional Garbage Out with the Trash!

Blow a Bubble, Not a Gasket!
Stress Management Techniques That Really Work

JOY: It's More Than a Detergent!
How to Trust Jesus in All Circumstances

Humor For Life!
Celebrates Laughter as a Gift from God; Explores Humor in the Workplace

Normal Is Gone, And It Won't Be Back!
Coping With and Embracing Change

YOU SAID WHAT?!#$%?&#??
Communicating Effectively: Listening and Speaking, In That Order!

"God, Bless 'Em, Change 'Em, or TAKE 'EM!"
Strategies for Dealing with Difficult People

You Want Me To Believe WHAT!!??
How to Believe God's Word When We Do Not Understand His Ways

The Little Engine Did, And So Can You!!!
The Incredible Power of Optimism to Energize Life and Propel Organizations Forward

To Boldly Go Where Few Have Gone Before:
Leadership Skills for the 21st Century!!

For more information or to schedule an appearance, contact Janie.
Office: 601-607-2979 • Mobile: 601-613-8849
joyfullyjanie@aol.com • www.janiewalters.com

Also by Janie Walters

Blow a Bubble Not a Gasket
101 Ways to Reduce Stress and Add Fun to Your Life

"If you feel that you are not having as much joy and fun as you want in life, then this book is for you. Quit complaining and take action to create the quality of life you want. Use this fabulous collection of ideas to start enjoying life more today!"

—Jack Canfield, Co-creator of the *Chicken Soup for the Soul series*

5x7 • Paperbound • 230 pages • Illustrations • Price: $10.00

Save 25% when you order the set!

Order the Janie Walters 2-book set for only
$15.00!
(Reg. price: $10.00 each)

Two-book set includes:
Blow a Bubble Not a Gasket and **The Garbage Truck Comes on Tuesdays and Fridays**